"Our union is now complete; our constitution composed,
established and approved.
You are now the guardian of your own liberties."

-*Samuel Adams*

In loving memory of my parents
Alice and Dennis,
and my wife Mary Anne.

Thank you.

Contents

Preface

Having reached the age of 90 recently, with the help of the good Lord and many wonderful people, reflecting over the great life I've enjoyed such as marrying the love of my life Mary Anne Costello, being blessed by six remarkable children and their families, having the privilege of living and working in the United States, South America and Mexico and serving in the United States Marine Corps, I would like to share with the reader some of my thoughts in the following dated essays/commentaries and also share this message.

Today our nation, our Constitutional Republic, our "government of the people, by the people and for the people," is facing many challenges. They are both domestic and foreign. I am sure the reader can identify and prioritize this long list but I would like to focus on a critical issue identified by our third President Thomas Jefferson's quote, "All tyranny needs to gain a foothold is for people of good conscience to remain silent."

There is a constant blizzard of data, news, information, political opinion, advertising that hits our eyes, our ears impacting our emotions, our brain, even our foundational values. Of course, this onslaught of incoming data has been brought about by the relatively new vehicles of social media such as, on-line networking, Facebook, Twitter, Smart Phones, and the latest creation computer-generated, photorealistic 3D avatars. The traditional vehicles of TV, Radio and Print accelerate their timing and volume by their use of social media.

Unfortunately, along with this explosion of incoming "news", polls show its recipients are far less confident today than a few years ago about its accuracy and/or lack of bias. Fake news, formerly called propaganda, abounds. The onus is on "journalists" to report the truth. The greater onus is on the viewer, the listener, the reader to use his/her own God-given power of reason and good conscience to judge.

Fortunately, at times our brain, our reason tells us this "news" is irrelevant or wrong and we simply turn away. There are other times this particular incoming seriously violates what you have learned, what you believe, what you support and you say "someone should say/do something about this." Make that someone you.

Now there are other times when there is no incoming about a cause/issue you believe in and your reason tells you "someone should say/do something" again you be that someone.

There needs to be a "grassroots", non-violent of course, counter-attack not only to all this avalanche of incoming but any censorship as well. The First Amendment guarantees the five freedoms; religion, speech, the press, assembly and petition. Let's use them. These "grassroots" patriots can use many of the same vehicles of social media, also telephone, letters, essays, personal visits etc. For example, you can contact your local, state or federal representative, you can join an internet community, a local organization or support a candidate who shares your views, engage in civil discourse with those who may not share your views, call the national TV channel or its local affiliate, contact advertisers, etc.

America needs an informed, educated, pro-active citizenry. A red-flashing warning signal is the abysmal voter turnout in our local, state and federal elections. As imperfect as we all are, including our elected politicians, an apathetic, non-participating citizenry is the greatest danger to the continued future and success of our Constitutional Republic.

Let me close by quoting a few lines from Thomas Paine's "Crisis" which was read to George Washington's troops on December 23, 1776, two days before the heroic crossing of the Delaware and the victory at Trenton.

"These are times that try men's souls. The summer soldiers and the sunshine patriot will in this crisis shrink from the service of their country, but he that stands it now deserves the love and thanks of man and woman. Tyranny like hell is not easily conquered; yet we have this consolation the harder the conflict the more glorious the triumph!"

A cursory look back at the 20th century: 1900-2000

March 22, 2018

The good news is the population of the United States during those 100 years grew from 76 million to 282 million. Also, the good news along with this huge increase in population was that people's average life span increased from about 47 years in 1900 to 77 years in 2000.

The 20th Century could be called the Age of Creativity and Invention or perhaps the Age of Better Things for More People. Just to mention a few:

1. <u>Agricultural Production</u> more than kept pace with the increases in population due mainly to mechanization, chemicals and science. Norman Borlaug, receiver of the Nobel Peace Prize, has been called the Father of "The Green Revolution" for the huge increase in the world's food supply due to his work.

2. <u>Clean Water</u> treatment, disinfection, filtration, chlorination caused major decreases in rates of mortality and disease. For example, typhoid fever cases of about 100 per 100,000 people in early 1900 dropped to less than 1 per 100m by the year 2000.

3. <u>Health & Medical</u>, miracle developments in vaccines, antibiotics, drugs, childbirth, surgical techniques, Alexander Fleming's discovery of penicillin in 1928 changed the course of medicine, Dr. Jonas Salk discovery of the Salk vaccines in 1955 to combat raging polio epidemics reducing upwards of 50,000 new cases a year in America to a mere handful.

4. <u>Energy</u>, fossil fuels, coal, oil and natural gas, petrochemicals, nuclear power, electricity generation and distribution. Fossil fuels played a critical role being the major source of the energy needed for a growing America. A large part of this demand for energy was to generate electricity. 20th century America was when the "lights (electric that is) came on".

5. <u>Transportation</u>, automobiles, airplanes, space ships. The Wright Brothers in 1903 flew the first successful powered airplane, staying aloft 12 seconds and flying 120'. Before the 20th century was over not only were there tens of thousands of jet planes but space ships circling the globe and American astronauts walking on the moon.

6. <u>Computers,</u> transistors, confirmation of Moore's Law. The first practical transistor was invented in 1947 by physicists John Bardeen, Walter Brattan

and William Shockley. They shared the Nobel Prize for Physics in 1956.

7. <u>DNA</u>, in 1953 after many years of work and help by other scientists James Watson and Francis Crick discovered the structure of DNA and how it carries genetic information. They called the event "the secret of life".

Yes, the 20th Century was the age of good news and the U. S. was a major contributor. With the remarkable outpouring and foundation of good news in the last century the 21st century should see an acceleration of good news.

Unfortunately, the 20th Century was also the age of bad news. The dark clouds of Communism, Nazism, and Shintoism began to gather in the early part of the century. A definition of terms is always important but for these three "isms" when you recall what destruction, devastation and deaths they caused you will know them. The two things they shared in common were their totalitarian suppression of human rights and their expansionist goals to infiltrate, conquer and rule over other countries. For the record brief definitions follow:

Communism, a political and economic ideology that believes society is a history of struggles between two classes, those who own capital, the bourgeois and those who work for those who have capital, not having any capital of their own, called the proletariat. This class struggle is directly caused by the capitalistic system and the capitalist class must be eliminated. The atheism of communism causes its leaders to inflict vicious, anti-religious actions against the religious. The genesis of communism was Karl Marx (1818-1883) who preached, "Communism begins when atheism begins" also "Religion is the opiate of the masses". A committed Marxist, Vladimir Lenin (1870-1924) was the leader who turned Russia into the Communist state Union of Soviet Socialist Republics (USSR) stated, "We do not believe in God. There is nothing more abominable than religion."

By the mid-1970s many countries, about 1/3 of the world's population (1.5 billion people) were under the yoke of communism, and their people were living under despotic tyrants who not only denied them their basic human rights but killed them for refusing to accept their dictates. Joseph Stalin (1879-1953), communist dictator of the Soviet Union from the late

1920s until his death in 1953 conducted his reign of terror for a quarter of the century, known for his ruthlessness, and killing tens of millions. Mao Zedong communist dictator of China with his "Great Leap Forward" killed even more than Stalin. There were many other countries whose leaders embraced communism. North Korea's communist dictator Kim ll Sung (grandfather of present NK dictator Kim Jong Un) after getting support from Stalin of the Soviet Union and Mao of China invaded South Korea starting the Korean War (1950-1953). North Vietnam's communist dictator Ho Chi Minh was a worthy contemporary of Stalin and Mao with his ruthless massacres of thousands of dissenters. His invasion of South Vietnam started the Vietnam War (1961-1975). The actual number is unknown but it has been estimated that during the 20th century, the totalitarian/dictators of communist countries caused over 100 million deaths of their own innocent, non-combatant people.

Nazism, a racist, anti-Semitic, fascist ideology that says the state is absolute, all citizens must follow the state, the Aryan race is superior to all other races and the state must actively promote the perfect race. This National-Socialist political/ economic system was initiated in the 1930's in Germany under the dictator Adolf Hitler. Hitler's rise to dictator of Germany was achieved by the Nazis using deprivation of human rights, violence, terror tactics and deception, while some Germans believed Hitler's promises, many of the non-Nazis were silent, or too weak/few to overcome the Nazis armed assaults. Germany began to militarily invade, conquer its neighboring countries and to kill millions of non-combatants, including more than six million Jews in Hitler's death camps as part of his anti-Semitic genocide goal of eliminating the Jewish race. The rest of the world looked on benignly as Germany under Hitler committed these atrocities and invasions.

Upon Germany's invasion of Poland in September 1939 the United Kingdom, France, Australia, India and New Zealand declared war on Germany, thus the beginnings of World War II. Many other countries, including the United States publicly declared their neutrality.

Shintoism, also called State Shinto, stems from the ancient Shinto religion, which held that the Japanese Emperor was divine, a descendant of the Sun Goddess Amaterasu, and had to be worshipped and obeyed. Shintoism also taught that the Japanese people were a special race of people whose divine purpose was to expand its power and tenets to other inferior races. Japan's national flag is the Hinomaru (circle of the rising sun) embodying Japan as the Land of the Rising Sun.

Under Emperor Hirohito in the early 20th century extreme nationalists and the military created State Shinto, a government sponsored/controlled religion. Military leaders would even dress in priestly Shinto ceremonial robes to conduct ritualistic ceremonies indoctrinating their people in the doctrines of State Shinto, including suppression of individual freedoms, contempt for other races, need to invade and conquer their Asian neighbors using any and all means of brutality, cruelty and terrorism. Japan's invasion of China in the 1930s was a calculated, planned attack of savagery, including rape and murder of non-combatants. The Rape of Nanking in 1937 epitomizes Japan's horrific, demonic, criminal war actions.

Japan attacked the United States on December 7, 1941 without warning by bombing Pearl Harbor, Hawaii. The Japanese planes emblazoned with the Hinomaru flag. The words "Remember Pearl Harbor" will forever echo across America. The United States immediately declared war on Japan, with President Roosevelt proclaiming Dec 7, 1941 as "a date that will live in infamy," four days later Germany (Dictator Hitler) declared war on the United States, later that day the United States (President Roosevelt) declared war on Germany. What was to become the largest and bloodiest war in history, World War II (1939-1945), was now officially underway. The second largest war in history World War I (1914-1918) had ended just 20 years earlier. As World War I raged the Muslim Ottoman-Turkish government under Islamic law committed the Armenian Genocide, killing millions of non-Muslims (mostly Christians). The 20th century could be called the century of wars and genocides.

In 1945 the Allies, under America's leadership forces, were victorious over the Axis powers (Germany, Japan, Italy). With the defeat of Germany and its leaders either dead or convicted and hung for their war crimes, Nazism was now eliminated. With the defeat of Japan and its leaders either dead or convicted and hung for their war crimes Shintoism was now eliminated. In Japan's case the unconditional surrender terms included the requirement that Emperor Hirohito deny he was a divinity and the Shinto religion would no longer be the state sponsored, controlled religion but would be a matter of personal choice.

After WWII Communist Soviet Union under Josef Stalin began an aggressive expansion foreign policy, tightening its control over Eastern Europe, actively supporting the Communist takeover of China by Mao Zedong in 1949, causing what was called the "Cold War" against its former allies the United States and Britain. The Soviet Union blocked the allies from entering their zones in Berlin (Berlin was deep inside Soviet occupied Germany); resulting in a massive airlift of food, coal medicines during 1948-49 by the allies for the over 2 million entrapped suffering and starving Berliners. The history of the airlift, a truly amazing story, is now largely forgotten. Eventually because thousands of persecuted East Germans were risking their lives fleeing their oppressors, the Soviets built what was called the "Berlin Wall" in the early 1960s. This wall was eventually torn down in 1989 because of the will and desire for freedom of the East Germans and the pressure to do so by the U. S. under President Ronald Reagan.

Islamism was the fourth "ism" reemerging force-fully in the 20th century. Islamism is the doctrinal, active promulgation of the religion of Islam, founded by the prophet Muhammad (570-632). The word Islam means submission without opposition, the word Muslim means one who submits. Muhammad was a man of war saying Allah their God commanded them to take up arms. Islamism is a totalitarian ideology whose goal is to change society in accordance with the law prescribed by Islam called Sharia Law by violence and terrorism. This change includes the elimination of not only non-Muslim's civil rights but also their beliefs and cultural influences. It's instructive to read the following from Page 362 of "The 9/11 Commission Report", "But the enemy is not just 'terrorism', some generic evil. The catastrophic threat is more specific. It is the threat posed by ISLAMIST terrorism."

Islamist terrorists attacked New York City (World Trade Center) and Washington DC (Pentagon) on 9/11/2001. The words "Remember 9/11" will forever echo across America. The 4th plane headed for the Capitol Building was forced to crash in a field in Pennsylvania by some heroic passengers who gave the message "Let's Roll" before they jumped the hijackers. This entire Islamist attack was planned by Osama bin Laden leader of Al Qaeda in the late 1990s. He was also responsible for the two Islamist terrorist bombings of America's embassies in Tanzania and Kenya in 1998 killing over 200 people. There were numerous Islamist Terrorist attacks around the world, including the U. S. Marine barracks in the 1983 killing over 200 marines and the original attack on the world Trade Center in 1993.

America, with huge sacrifices by its military forces and its civilians on the home front, was the giant protector of the world during the 20th century against those evil "isms" that caused such horrific bad news throughout the century. Those evil forces had an enormous debilitating impact on what could have been even more good news. One can only imagine how much better off billions of people would have been at the close of the 20th century had those evil 20th century leaders not chosen racism, denial of human rights, expansion, totalitarianism and other incredible evils but rather those principle truths "that all men are created equal, that they are endowed by their Creator with certain unalienable Rights, that among these are Life, Liberty and the pursuit of Happiness".

The evil "isms" of Communism and Islamism are still with us as we enter the 21st century. The threats posed by Russia, China, North Korea along with Islamism are huge and will require America and other countries of the free world to promote and protect freedom. Freedom was not free in the 20th century, nor will it be free in the 21st century.

Thank you to the United States military for their service and sacrifices

April 22, 2018

Each century of America's existence, since its first war beginning April 19, 1775 at the Battle of Lexington and Concord against the British forces, has been marked by major wars with America fighting for its rights and liberty. That date is now honored as Patriots' Day.

The 13 American colonies at the time had a population of about 2.5 million. Estimates vary but about 10% of the population, enlisted and militia, served during the entire war. America was clearly the underdog against the world power Great Britain. The American War Library (AWL) reports over 25,000 killed, 8,000 wounded. After 6 years of incredible sacrifice by the military and civilians, the new nation, the United States of America (as declared on July 4, 1776 by the 2nd Continental Congress) won its freedom.

Even though this was a great victory it would take 6 more years until September 17, 1787 for the Founding Fathers to create and adopt the new, unique, unprecedented system of federal government called The

Constitution of the United States. The Revolutionary War was the 1ˢᵗ critical step for the birth of our nation.

The next existential crisis for this new nation, not yet 100 years old, was the Civil War (1861-1865). The United States had a population of about 31 million with 22 million on the Union side and 9 million on the Confederate side. Union military numbered over 2 million, the Confederates over 1 million. The AWL reports the Union suffered 363,000 deaths and 281,000 wounded, the Confederates suffered 199,000 deaths and 137,000 wounded, making America's total deaths and wounded 3% of the population, by far the greatest casualty rate of all America's wars.

The over-riding cause of the Civil War was slavery. Slavery was legal and well established in the 13 colonies before the Revolutionary War. It was restricted to those with African roots who could neither vote nor own property. Northern states began publicly opposing slavery, promoting and enacting abolitionist laws. The Southern states resisted these abolitionist movements. The North-South enmity was further inflamed by the U.S. Supreme Court's outrageous 7-2 Dred Scott decision in 1857 declaring the negro slave Dred Scott, was property and could be bought/sold/owned like other property. Shortly after Abraham Lincoln's election in 1860 the growing hostilities regarding slavery resulted in seven Southern states seceding from the United States. The Confederate forces fired on the Union soldiers at Ft. Sumter, S.C in 1861 beginning America's military civil war. Abraham Lincoln's Presidency, his decisions, his actions, his leadership resulted in a Union victory and preservation of the United States of America.

There were five major wars in the 20th century, World War I (1917-1918), World War II (1941-1945), Korean War (1950-1953), Vietnam War (1961-1975), Desert Shield-Storm (1990-1991).

WORLD WAR I, population in 1920, 106 million, military size 4.7 million 4.4% of population, military deaths 117,000, wounded 204,000, ttl casualties 321,000

WORLD WAR II, population in 1940, 132 million, military size 16.1 million 12.2% of population, military deaths 408,000, wounded 671,000, ttl casualties 1,076,000

KOREAN WAR, population in 1950, 151 million, military size 5.7 million 3.8% of population, military deaths 54,000, wounded 103,000, ttl casualties 157,000

VIETNAM WAR, population in 1970, 203 million, military size 8.7 million 4.3% of Population, military deaths 65,000, wounded 153,000, ttl casualties 218,000

DESERT SHIELD/STORM, pop. in 1990, 249 million, mil. Size 2.3 million 0.9% of Population, military deaths 363, wounded 357, ttl casualties 720

SPECIAL NOTE: above numbers from American War Library and U.S. Dept of Veteran's Affairs titled "America's Wars" see for relevant footnotes.

Essays and Commentary ...

Following are some dated essays and commentary over the past 25 years with the author "speaking up" on the issues of the day.

1. 'Manufacturing environmentalism'

April 11, 1993

If we don't save New York's factories, we may all be looking for work

For 20 years, whether the national economy was in recession, boom or recovery, New York state manufacturing jobs have been declining. Since 1970 we have been in a state of free fall in loss of manufacturing jobs.

Although we need desperately to add manufacturing jobs, New York would indeed be fortunate if it could only slow the rate of decline so the state could exit this decade at 850,000 manufacturing jobs. That's half the 1970 levels.

A critical factor in the economy of New York state is the ratio of manufacturing jobs to government jobs. Unfortunately, that relationship is deteriorating at an alarming rate.

As you can see from the following graph, the number of government jobs in New York moved ahead of the number of manufacturing jobs in the 1980s, and the gap continues to widen. Not only are the government jobs increasing but their rates of pay and benefits are too, at a higher percentage than wages and benefits in the manufacturing sector.

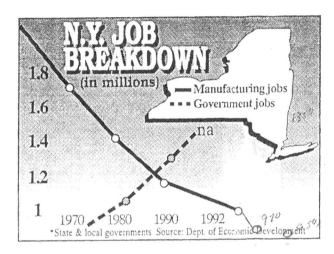

Were we to establish a rule that "government jobs cannot exceed 77 percent of manufacturing jobs" (the 1980 relationship), the level of government jobs in 1992 would be 755,000 nearly a half-million fewer than we had in 1990!

Is it an arbitrary rule? Yes, but it could be "a stake in the ground" to measure performance. The fact is the level of government jobs can no longer be disconnected from levels of private sector jobs, its major emphasis being manufacturing.

The economy's engine

Let's reflect for a moment on exactly what manufacturers are, what they do, and what they create.

- New York's manufacturers drive the state's economy forward with a multiplier effect far higher than any other economic activity.
- Wealth is not created by endless legislative sessions in Albany, by selling shoes made out of the country, or by transferring assets from one account to another (banking). The manufacturers and farmers are responsible for creating New York's wealth.
- Manufacturers hold the key to the innovations and improved products most likely to improve New York state's economic future.
- As the manufacturing sector is vital to the economic health of our nation, so too is it vital to New York state. It is axiomatic that every unnecessary new cost imposed on them makes our products less competitive in the global marketplace. When New York manufacturers lose orders because of a lack of competitiveness, New York workers lose their jobs.

New York state leads the nation both in the tax burden on its residents and in the rate of government spending. This is not news to most residents and certainly not to our governmental jurisdictions, representatives and appointees. It is clear the level of taxes and size of government are having a disastrous impact on our economy and the well-being of our citizens.

Our great Empire State is reaching a perilous condition of economic dry-rot. The game is not over but it is definitely in the fourth quarter and the game plan needs drastic changing. Each of us will have to get into the game with total focus on the goals.

Simply put, those goals are:

- To design and enact a culture of "manufacturing environmentalism" across the state.
- To reduce the size and cost of local and state government, while at the same time improving its quality of performance.

Manufacturing environmentalism

Let's talk first about "manufacturing environmentalism." In order to place New York's economy in the proper perspective, we need to accept as a fact the animal known as "manufacturing" is on the endangered species list.

We could start by changing the mind-set of the media and academia toward industrial activity. Manufacturing plants are only newsworthy if a pollution suit is involved, or if some other form of bad news arises. We have to convince the opinion-molders that manufacturing and good news are not mutually exclusive. Only then can the hostile environment that has been created for manufacturing become a friendly habitat that can sustain the species.

Any manufacturing environmentalism movement would have to be broadly based and incorporate all the nuts and bolts of any good environmental effort.

Those individuals who invest and work in manufacturing, from entry level to CEO, need to be given high status and recognition that they are the engine, the "breadwinners" who are satisfying the needs of the people and providing the financial strength for future growth and well-being.

Cutting government

Concerning the size and structure of New York state government, the time for token effort or minor surgery is long past. We need to perform major surgery on the archaic, counter-productive bureaucratic structures, state and local. Bureaucracies inexorably increase in size, cost and ineffectiveness. Much like weeds in a garden, they need to be continuously purged in order to permit innovation and creativity.

A prime example of a bloated bureaucracy is the state's primary and secondary education structure. This is an area where New York is one of the nation's largest spenders with woefully inadequate results. Studies have shown that based on annual expenditures of $8,600 per pupil, we spend 58 percent more than the national average! Despite this profligate spending our education establishment continues to demand more money.

Contributors to this bureaucratic labyrinth include: the state Education Department, Board of Regents, Senate Education Committee and Sub-committees, Assembly Education Committee and Sub-committee, district superintendents, school principals, teachers' unions, National Education Association, American Federation of Teachers, lobbying groups, consulting firms, and various associations with geographical subchapters.

Pressures for change are causing "turf battles" to erupt among these administrative dinosaurs because they are sensing rapidly diminishing philosophical as well as taxpayer support for their continued existence. However, we cannot expect members of these groups to support basic cultural change. After all, they have a vested interest in the status quo. Change will only come from those New Yorkers outside the establishment.

Many fundamental changes are needed. For example:

- Consolidation of the more than 700 school districts across the state as well as the downsizing of the Education Department in Albany by transferring administrative and budget functions to the local level. Such a restructuring would begin the process to develop real local control and diversity, which is essential as we enter the 21st century.

- Across-the-board wage cuts of 10 percent as well as a 10 percent reduction of personnel. Combined with this there should be a longer school day with the school year extended to 240 days.

- A phase-out of the vast majority of those positions across in the bureaucracy that do not come in contact with students. The first priority for major purging should be the positions in Albany.

There are many areas of opportunity in our state and local government for downsizing and performance improvement. Hopefully, each of us in our relations with our public servants will challenge rather than acquiesce, be assertive rather than conciliatory, and participate vigorously in the process.

2. Government waste begins at home

October 23, 1994

Instead of blaming Albany and Washington, local officials ought to cut waste in local governments first

New York residents pay the highest taxes in the nation. This is not exactly a late-breaking news item. We know this because of the continuous drumbeat of news reports over the years including Money magazine's now-famous characterization of New York as a "tax hell."

A large part of the reason for this is local government (county, towns, school districts, cities, villages). Obviously, we cannot ignore state and federal impacts. However, there is, within the myriad of local governments (over 11,000 statewide) a great need for changes.

There are many opportunities for local governments to eliminate redundancies, introduce new arrangements, consolidate services and to develop better government at less cost. These opportunities are in no way restricted or even impeded by Albany or Washington. On the other hand, there are no shortages of reasons (excuses?) for local government leaders to maintain the status quo and to avoid the trauma of change.

Hired public officials in administration and in public unions have for too long intimidated our elected officials by invoking the power of the state as the reason for their resistance to change. Elected officials tend to go along with their administrators because, after all, the professionals are the "experts." Elected officials need to exercise leadership and be responsive to their constituencies when they call for better government at less cost. They need to conquer their lack of confidence and get on with the task.

Let's take a moment and look at Ontario County as an economic and social unit, a community if you will, of 95,000 people. This community consists of a number of governmental jurisdictions: the county, 16 towns, ten school districts, eight villages, two cities and many water districts, drainage districts, etc. The annual budgets for all these public jurisdictions combined will approach $400 million next year. That's about $4,000 for each man, woman and child living in Ontario County.

The school districts alone account for about one-half of the total. With a county-wide enrollment of

20,000, this is an annual cost per student of $10,000. These ten school districts have ten superintendents along with their respective administrative staffs and other non-teaching departments. There is no justification for either the size or cost of this administrative bureaucracy.

It seems as if all the jurisdictions in the county are beating the drums for more revenue through sales tax, income tax and property tax. The levels of these taxes have seriously eroded the discretionary income of virtually all our residents, with the most devastating impact being felt by those who can least afford it, namely young families starting out and senior citizens on fixed income.

The other victim is jobs, especially private sector jobs.

It is clear that the private sector in Ontario County is experiencing a devastating decrease in its discretionary income. The public sector on the other hand is insulated because its income rises faster than the cost of living and its benefits are paid for by the taxpayer.

If one looks around Ontario County one can only be struck by the enormous opportunities for simplification, re-engineering, downsizing, or demassifying (pick out the word of your choice) our local governments.

How do Ontario County's elected leaders, all of whom would agree with the goal of better government at less cost, begin the process? There are two concepts that should be the cornerstones of such a process: privatization and consolidation.

Let's first talk about consolidation. This is no doubt one of the longest running subjects of discussion and study in and about New York political circles. It is probably second only to the subject of weather and like the weather nothing much is ever done about it.

Locally, the areas of opportunity lie in consolidating the functions of administration, personnel, computer operations, purchasing, highways, motor pools, law enforcement to name only a few. It's encouraging to note the success of consolidation efforts vis a vis the county's 911 service. However, much more is needed and much more is possible.

Privatization is a relatively new way of looking at producing and arranging for the delivery of services to the general public. The essential characteristic of privatization is it views producing a service and arranging for its delivery as two separate issues.

Some people express concern about the "P" word, privatization, because they immediately see governmental services as being turned over to the uncaring, profit-driven private sector. Wrong! A broad and diverse range of city and county services are being contractually produced by private firms across the country. Some 180 "governmental" services, including computer operations, solid waste disposal, vehicle fleet management, buildings and ground maintenance and jail operations can be performed better and cheaper by private firms.

The city of Hartford, Conn. has just recently arranged for a private concern, Education Alternatives Inc. (EAl), to run its entire school system. EAI's philosophy is "The problem in public schools is not the people in them, but rather the system itself. We believe that as personnel in the schools become the decision-makers, they will spend more money in the classroom and less on overhead."

It is a given the privatization and consolidation roads are difficult, but the potential rewards are substantial. Let's get on with it.

3. Rural areas differ greatly from Monroe

February 7, 1996

The Democrat and Chronicle continuously - and in my view, erroneously - performs economic analyses for the "Rochester Metro Area," defined as, the counties of Monroe, Wayne, Ontario, Livingston, Orleans, and Genesee.

The fact is that the five rural counties have substantially different economic profiles and relationships from those of Monroe County.

A December 31 "Economic Forecast" and other, more recent articles failed to even mention agricultural factors and trends, sharp declines in the number of farms, acres harvested and market value of agricultural products at the producer level all have had a serious adverse economic impact, not only on those directly involved in farming, but on supporting businesses.

Total annual payroll dollars for public sector jobs (federal, state, school, county, city, town, village) for 1994 in the five rural counties were nearly 50 percent of the total annual payroll dollars in the private sector. The comparable public-sector share in Monroe County is less than 15 percent.

Both in Monroe County and the five rural counties, private sector payroll dollars are decreasing in relation to inflation, while public sector payroll dollars are increasing at two to three times that rate.

The 40 percent increase in the late eighties for school wages in Monroe County has not only had a ripple impact on school wages in the five rural counties, but also on other local public wages.

As a result of this ripple effect of pay increases in the public sector, there's very little difference in Monroe's total wages and benefits compared with rural counties. However, private sector wages in Monroe County average about 50 percent higher in the five rural counties.

Public sector employees in the rural counties, with generous wages and Cadillac non-contributing fringe - benefit plans are truly the affluent group.

Regressive taxes such as sales tax, property tax and gross receipts tax, along with greater-than-inflation increases in essentials such as utilities, are having a devastating impact on low-wage private sector employees.

Public sector employees are a protected class and insulated from this negative effect because of their substantially higher and rising wage and benefit levels.

Exorbitant taxes inhibit new and existing businesses and darken the economic horizon. Industrial, agricultural and other businesses are demanding and getting tax relief in order to remain competitive and stay in business.

These tax exemptions simply throw greater tax burdens on the already overburdened individual taxpayer; unless the cost of government is reduced.

This gets back to the issue of wages and benefits in the public sector in the rural counties. At the local government level, the great amount of dollars in annual budgets are for wages and benefits of employees. For example, about 80 percent of school budgets are made up of wages and benefits.

It is abundantly clear that rural counties, in order to revitalize their economies, must start to reduce taxes. To begin to reduce taxes, it is mandatory that rural counties in upstate New York begin to downsize public sector payrolls.

The Democrat and Chronicle's economic forecast stated that "jobs in the Rochester area are linked to growth of overall U.S. economy. If the national economy slumps the Rochester area slumps." A case could be made, based on history, that if the national economy slumps, rural upstate communities "slump more", and if the national economy grows, upstate counties "merely slump".

I commend your attempts to forecast the Rochester-area economy. However, I suggest you go back to the drawing board and develop a more rigorous, in-depth analysis of the five rural counties.

I urge you to include data and trends in agriculture, diverging public sector wages and benefits vs. those in the private sector and all taxes, among others.

4. Vote is here; districts must make changes

August 21, 1996

The state Senate and Assembly have passed and the governor has signed into law legislation giving the right to vote on school budgets to citizens of the 57 small-city school districts.

This is a well-deserved victory for those who, in grass-roots efforts across the state, signed petitions, sent postcards, made phone calls or personally visited their state representatives, and they are to be congratulated.

Those senators and assemblymen who voted for the right to vote also are to be congratulated.

Those who supported the right to vote are obligated to continue to be informed, to communicate with our school officials, to evaluate options and, obviously, to cast our votes. Gaining this very important democratic privilege should inspire us to more fully participate in the process.

Members of school administrations, boards and teachers' unions across the state, some of whom may have been anti-vote, are obligated to respond to this new law in a positive, constructive manner. The implementation of this new legislation will require some immediate changes in the processes of budgeting, voting and communication.

Over the longer term, it can be expected that cultural changes will evolve as a result of this new partnership between school officials and the customers they serve.

For example, Canandaigua City School District officials should begin to develop a plan of implementation, to include:

- Education for residents of the school district, including terms and conditions of the new law as well as responsibilities and consequences.

- Open up and publicize the new budget process so as to give visibility and specificity to the budget as related to the voting rights law, such items as fully allocated administrative spending, facilities operation and maintenance, transportation, labor contracts, debt and debt service, trend analysis data and options for new ways to deliver better results at lower costs.

- Develop formal voting control procedures for registration, eligibility, access, monitoring and recording.

Increase the number of polling places. The single voting booth in the elementary school literally denies access to upwards of 12,000 voters in a school district whose footprint is 15 miles long by 10 miles wide, impacting five towns and the city of Canandaigua. Distribute maps detailing district boundaries, demographics, voting locations. Format the voting issues compatibly with the changed budget process.

In summary, there is reason for optimism regarding implementation of the voting rights law. However, a note of caution is warranted.

A state-by-state survey of lobbying laws by the New York Public Interest Group reports that New York has one of the weakest lobbying laws in the nation.

The number of registered lobbyists in Albany has quadrupled in the past two decades. The amount of money spent on lobbying increases every year, by 17 percent in 1995, for example.

At the forefront of those lists of lobbyists are the education lobbyists, with the state's main teachers union (New York State United Teachers) leading the pack and whose spending is more than three times that of its closest rivals.

These full-time educational lobbyists in Albany were relentless in their efforts to defeat this voting rights legislation. They lost, but they are still there and are more powerful than ever.

It will be an uphill battle for those of us who want to more fully participate in the process to persuade our school officials to change, to move their organizational structures and administrative approaches into the 21st century, so we can jointly begin to bring school costs into line with economic resources.

5.   N.Y. should trim its costs and cut taxes

March 12, 1997

New York state has won the tax Super Bowl for the fifth year in a row, according to the January Money magazine. It has scored highest of all 50 states.

In fact, New York taxes are 20 percent to 50 percent higher than those of the bordering states of Massachusetts, Connecticut, Pennsylvania, New Jersey and Vermont. The state's taxes are 38 percent higher than California's.

The primary reasons for the state's high taxes are the astronomically high costs generated by state and local governments in providing services. The largest part of this cost is public sector jobs. Public sector jobs, wages and benefits are rising at three times the rate of inflation, while private sector jobs are falling behind the inflation rate.

For example, local public-sector wages in Ontario County soared 29 percent from 1991 to 1995, according to the state Labor Department. Continuing this trend and adding fringe benefits such as retirement will bring the total to more than $300 million by 2000.

The executive and legislative branches in Albany, perennial underachievers, continue to be overstaffed and overcompensated. Their performance, by any measure, is a disgrace to the citizens of our state.

Private sector workers with diminishing jobs, wages and benefits are taxed higher and higher to pay for growing public sector jobs, wages and benefits. The most damaging forms of taxation are the regressive taxes on human needs, namely property taxes on homes, sales taxes on clothing and gross receipts taxes and sales taxes on utilities. All taxes, direct and indirect, are in the end paid by real people.

There has been a Niagara of words out of Albany about lowering taxes, but hardly a murmur about legislative action to begin to lower the cost of providing state and local governmental services. A good place to start would be reforming New York's lobbying laws, which are among the nation's weakest.

An accelerating torrent of lobbying dollars flow into Albany. Documented lobbying expenditures reached $47 million in 1995, a 17 percent increase over 1994. Reports for 1996 show lobbying dollars running well ahead of 1995's record pace. At this rate, lobbying dollars will easily top $100 million in 2000.

When it comes to state lobbying, the 2,000-pound gorilla is the New York State United Teachers union. By far the biggest spender in lobbying wars, it spends at three times the rate of No.2, the Public Employees Union. Then come the Civil Service Employees Association, the state's bankers and trial lawyers.

At last count there were more than 1,900 registered lobbyists in the state. You, John Q. Private Citizen, are not one of them, so go to the end of the line. Just remember, only high-stakes games are played here.

In The Wall Street Journal recently, the former chairman of the state's Urban Development Corp. said that the list of lobbyists and contributors to statewide and legislative campaigns is "a who's who of special interests". Large campaign contributors who profit royally from the state's dysfunctional policies include PACs of financial institutions that do business with and are regulated by the state.

"According to Moody's Investor Service, an astonishing 40 percent of the entire nation's outstanding municipal debt is in New York state and local bonds. The public finance departments of Wall Street, New York's merchants of debt; have an enormous financial stake in heavy state spending and borrowing and amount to a vast welfare program for the affluent."

Also, we need laws that:

- Allow free and open management of public sector employees. This objective, no doubt, is the toughest because of public sector unions' power. However, the "right to manage" must be restored to elected representatives on governing boards.

- Impose strong ethics rules to help representatives exercise their consciences when dealing with the sycophants of government.

- Ensure that the deregulation now under way for public utilities results in lower prices and taxes for residential customers.

- Create incentives to eliminate obsolete government agencies and operations. We should combine redundant operations, privatize where beneficial and use new technology to reduce costs.

State and local representatives have to match their rhetoric with action. Only by cutting the cost of providing government service can we reduce the level of taxes.

States across the nation are racing to govern efficiently and effectively with lower taxes. New York state continues to fall behind.

6. Time to lay government consolidation on the table

December 8, 1997

I have read with great interest recent articles in the Democrat and Chronicle about the need for local governments in New York state to consolidate and share resources. The articles contained much with which I concur, and that I even applaud.

Some considerations as this discussion continues, are:

- The cost-benefit opportunities are enormous for the consolidation of local government functions.
- There is no need to cut services provided by local governments but rather to devise more cost-effective and efficient methods of delivering "those services".
- The true amount of grassroots support for change and real solutions is unknown, because of all the mixed and "anti-change" messages of special interests and lobbyists.
- There is a need to communicate to the community. clear, consistent, candid, persuasive and re-

petitive answers to the "what, why, how; who and when" of achieving consolidation.

Rochester Mayor William Johnson Jr.'s spirited call to "reduce the spiraling costs of government… because all of upstate New York is dying" is a message that needs to be heard and acted upon.

It's important to keep in mind that any substantial cost reduction will result in "downsizing" local public-sector jobs.

As we continue to fail to achieve government cost reductions" residents and businesses will continue to pay increasing taxes. This outcome must be a key part of any dialogue surrounding these issues, including the need to return to our elected representatives the right to manage and control public sector employees."

Private sector real income and benefits have been declining whereas public sector jobs, income and benefits have been increasing at three times the rate of inflation.

Public sector employees have become the new privileged class in New York state.

Consolidation among school districts of non-instructional functions also would put more dollars into the classrooms. Shockingly, public schools maintain a nearly 1-to-1 ratio, teachers to overseers, compared to the 7-to-1 ratio in private schools.

The dialogue on consolidation also needs to include the privatization of various public-sector functions, charter schools and school vouchers.

There is an accelerating, even. desperate rush by local governments to extend grants, tax credits, low utility rates, loans and other incentives in J the name of industrial and commercial development.

These efforts are justifiable in many cases due to the seriously non-competitive nature of New York state. However, as we continue to fail to achieve real cost reduction in government operations, residents and existing businesses will continue to pay increasing taxes.

Print media can be the best vehicle for communicating objective, comprehensive messages on these very complex issues provided they can correct the public's perception that they're biased.

The anti-change lobbyists have the podium, the money, the PR expertise and the ability to get their message into the print and TV media. Right now there is no comparable source for countervailing messages.

The print media in upstate New York in a collaborative of their own and in partnership with other members of the private and public sectors should initiate a continuing information and education program on local government, its key players, databases/trends, plans and performance.

This information could be published in a semiannual or annual "textbook." Ideally these textbooks would be released across the state at the same time.

Unfortunately, Albany and entrenched local governments are not going to be the agents of change. It is time to draw grass-roots people into these critical issues.

A collaborative effort could be a major step in this direction.

7.   State education system suffering sclerosis

March 4, 2006

New York's governance at all levels, state, city, county and schools is afflicted with systemic sclerosis. Others, usually in the private sector, have called it a "calcified bureaucracy," a "union run monopoly" and a "regulatory nightmare."

Why use the term sclerosis? Sclerosis of the arteries is defined as a combination of arterial aging and fatty deposits making the arteries more cluttered, less flexible and capable of delivering the blood flow efficiently throughout the body. In the same sense as the arteries the purpose of statewide governance is to deliver services to the public. It's clear state governance at all levels is an aging, bloated bureaucracy and is in need of major lifestyle changes.

Let's focus on one very important segment of that governance.

The state's K-12 public education, organizationally, is still living in the mid-20th century. There are 700 school districts across the state, each with their own non-classroom overhead structures. In addition, there are 38 BOCES operations that alone spend billions.

There are tens of billions of dollars being spent on non-classroom overhead, which represents about half of all the billions spent.

The state Education Department projects a continuing decline in K-12 enrollment to 2.7 million in the fall of 2009. Enrollment in 1971 was 3.5 million. The 2004-05 "Facts and Figures" by the Four County School Board Association (Ontario, Seneca, Yates and Wayne) reports 15 school districts out of 19 with total enrollments declining by 4 percent from 2002-03 to 2004-05, some districts with declines of 7 to 11 percent. The combined staffs total 5,928 for total enrollment of 31,812 pupils, an overall ratio of 5.4 pupils per staff member. BOCES, itself, has an additional 1002 on staff.

If total statewide spending trend lines are projected, along with the recently settled State Court of Appeals decision, spending will double in about the next four years. State educrats say even this is not enough. They offer no solution but higher property and income taxes. What is the answer?

K-12 public education needs 21st century organization, entrepreneurial management, meritocracy concepts, redistricting, consolidation of overheads, distance learning, diversity of school systems and to throw out the hierarchical structures. With 21st century organization and governance tens of billions could be diverted to more time in the classrooms, more investment in new curriculums for math and science, greater choice for parents and pupils and maybe even a small portion returned to the taxpayers.

The dysfunction of governance in public education is replicated in state, city and county governments.

New York must reduce the cost of delivery of services. According to the Citizens Budget Commission report of April 2005 on 2004 data, "the hourly earnings of state and local government employees (no benefits included) exceed those of the private sector in the greater New York City region by an average of 15 percent." Commission President Diana Fortuna says, " ... the fact public sector wages exceed those of the private sector means that we must now all consider what levels of compensation the taxpayer should be asked to pay."

The New York State Department of Labor reports 2004 annual average wages for all public-sector jobs exceed those of all the private sector by these percentages in these counties: Ontario 20, Yates 35, Seneca 24 and Cayuga 41. If benefits are added the percentages become substantially greater. Such huge and growing disparities between the public sector and the diminishing private sector are simply not sustainable.

As "lifestyle changes" have taken hold in the private sector in recent years across the state, it is long past time that New York's public sector begin the process of major "lifestyle changes."

Such changes should take place along three major paths:

- Major reorganization for the 21st century.
- Fat reduction. If a public-sector employee is not in some way performing "hands-on" delivery of services that employee must be considered overhead and subject to "force reduction".
- A phased reduction of wages and benefits across all public employees.

The continuing decline of private sector jobs, wages and benefits, particularly in upstate New York demands no less.

8. How to cut state's high tax bill

September 25,2006

The residential property tax is an unfair, regressive tax. It violates the fundamental requirement that taxes be determined based on people's ability to pay. Skyrocketing property taxes combined with shrinking discretionary incomes have placed upstaters, particularly a large number of those in the private sector, in serious economic hardship.

Residents with low income spend a much higher percentage of their income to pay property taxes than those with high income. This disparity becomes even more egregious when varying federal income tax brackets are considered. Those with high taxable income can get up to a 35 percent offset on their property tax, compared to those with low taxable income getting only a 15 percent or less offset.

In an attempt to lessen such regressivity, state laws, justifiably, permit local school districts', counties, cities, towns and villages to exempt from 5 percent to 50 percent of the tax bill for those 65 or older. The current state law has a cap of $32,400. However, many jurisdictions unjustifiably maintain much lower income caps than allowed, thereby defeating the purpose of moderating regressivity, for many.

Local taxing jurisdictions should raise qualifying caps to state allowable levels.

The State Legislature and the governor should raise qualifying income levels to comparable rises in property taxes or inflation, whichever is greater.

The State Legislature and governor should make similar legislation for those under 65.

Local legislators say they can't do this because "We will lose revenue." Perish the thought one would ever suggest that politicians lose "tax revenue." So, let's look at two major property tax exemption loopholes that need to be closed to recover such "lost revenue".

An exemption that needs to be eliminated is what is referred to as the "Condo law." Section 339-y of the Condominium Act provides an assessment cap ceiling. Currently across the state there are many "condo" owners paying property taxes at as low as 25 percent to 40 percent of taxes for comparably valued regular individual residences. The State Legislature and the governor should repeal Real Property Tax Law S339-y so as to provide non-discriminatory treatment for all types of residential housing.

An operational weakness, which in effect results in major discriminatory assessments, is the fact that assessment rolls lag behind real market values. In rapidly appreciating housing, such as lake property, under-assessments not only result in underpayment but also cause the municipality to understate its total assessment value, thereby overstating its tax rate (same is true of Condo Law above). On the other hand, in declining housing over-assessments result in overpayment.

The State Legislature and the governor should enact legislation requiring local jurisdictions to place all relevant sales transaction, assessment and exemption data online, the cost to be reimbursed by the state.

The state's Real Estate Property Tax system, another one of the state's huge lumbering dinosaurs, will be collecting at an annual rate of $2,000 per capita in the year 2007. This is 50 percent higher than the national average.

Although this article's focus is on residential property taxes, it's important to remember commercial property tax machinations have a substantial impact on the final tax paid by individual residents.

This commercial side has its own tangled web of methodologies, preferences, exemptions, etc.

Ultimately all taxes are paid by the consumer. For example, property taxes and other taxes on utility bills add up to about 20 percent of the total bill. Taxes are a major reason why utility bills are so high in the state.

Over the years layer upon layer of exemptions, some justified, some not justified have been incorporated into the property tax system. It is highly likely property taxes will continue to increase. Therefore, state and local legislators have to rigorously take actions to continuously moderate inherent regressivity, and discrimination in the system. This would include removing many decades-old exemptions that are no longer justified.

Some have said, well let's just increase the tax brackets on income tax and get more money from mid to high-income residents. There are many reasons why this is not the right answer. One is those with higher incomes are the most mobile and do, as many have, and vote with their feet. Everyone knows New York State leads the nation in combined state and local taxes, over 50 percent higher than neighboring states such as Ohio and Pennsylvania, 68 percent over New Hampshire,25 percent over Massachusetts, running upwards of 70 percent to 80 percent over Florida, Georgia and Texas.

The final answer for New York State is to reduce the cost of delivering services by downsizing the public sector and switching the public sector from its mission of running the state for the benefit of the public sector to running the state for all the people.

9.   Fight them there, or fight them here

October 20, 2006

The Daily Messenger's editorial pages re: the national political scene have been a steady drumbeat of anti-Bush rhetoric. On Oct. 15 an editorial from the Los Angeles Times ridicules President Bush by saying he "insults our intelligence" when he referred recently to fighting the terrorists "over there" makes us safer "over here."

The president's remarks were in fact in the 9/11 Commission Report, (page 362) "Islamist terrorism against American interests 'over there' should be regarded just as we regard terrorism against American interests 'over here.' It can only be destroyed or utterly isolated." It's the Times' commentary that "insults our intelligence," not President Bush.

Terrorist leaders have repeatedly declared war on America, vowed elimination of Americans and America, declaring it is the duty of every Muslim to murder any Americans anywhere on earth, not differentiating between military and civilian. (page 47)

They have committed horrific acts of war against the U.S. for years including the 9/11 atrocities. The

United States of America is at war with Islamist terrorists in Afghanistan, in Iraq, in the United States and across the globe. It is the most important issue facing America.

In war there is no disaster greater than being disunited, misunderstanding and underestimating your enemy. Today a very vocal liberal left, embedded within academia, major news media and current leadership of the Democratic party, is dividing our nation and giving aid and comfort to our enemy.

Listen to Winston Churchill, "If you will not fight for the right when you can easily win without bloodshed, if you will not fight when your victory will be sure and not too costly, you may come to the moment when you will have to fight with all the odds against you and only a precarious chance of survival. There may even be a worse case. You may have to fight when there is no hope of victory, because it is better to perish than live as slaves."

Our president/commander-in-chief and our military are waging a courageous and effective war against the Islamist terrorists. They know the enemy. It is going to be a long and difficult struggle. They need the united, loyal support of Congress and of the. American people.

It is essential the American electorate reject those politicians who have been causing disunity and emboldening our enemy by voting against them in November.

10. Consolidating and downsizing the public sector in NY State

June 3, 2007

Governor Spitzer in his state of the state address made very strong commitments for reform. High on his list was to reform local government. He said, "We must consolidate New York's multiple layers of local government-those 4200 jurisdictions cost taxpayers millions each year in duplicative services and stand as yet another impediment to change. 4200 taxing jurisdictions are just too many, too expensive and too burdensome." Strong words, not that they haven't been said before by every New York State Governor over the past decades. Never the less I say yes to the Governor, but how about starting in your own backyard, Albany.

Headline stories for years are that Upstate New York's economy is bad and getting worse. Actually, this is only partially true because as we all know the public sector from Buffalo to Albany, from the Southern Tier to the St. Lawrence is doing very well with job, wage and benefits growth. The public sector is in fact good and getting better. It is the private sector that is bad and getting worse.

Is consolidation of State and local governmental operations the answer to reducing New York States "cost of government"?

Let's use the issue of consolidating the function of property assessments in Ontario County since New York State created a statewide consolidation aid incentive plan to do just that in 1994 when there were about 1200 separate municipal assessing units. According to the NYS Office of Real Property Services there are still about 1200 separate municipal assessing units in the state as compared to most other states with their limited number of county-level jurisdictions. Such a dismal lack of achievement would indicate one should not enter into such a venture with undue optimism.

First, we need to examine the New York state Real Property Tax systems, administration, and legalities. Remember we are dealing with both non-commercial(residential) and commercial.

Is it inefficient, unfair and broken as many claim?

Is it possible to peel back layer upon layer of archaic legislative actions, special preferences, exemptions, and dare I say it, political manipulations?

Are we not merely trying to collect more taxes more efficiently?

If we "consolidate" assessor's offices without substantive changes in operational practices/legalities, would that not be like changing the deck chairs on the Titanic?

Are we attacking only the symptoms and not the disease?

Property taxes are collected to pay for schools and local governments. Willie Sutton the infamous bank robber, when asked, Willie, why do you rob banks? He said, "Because that's where the money is". In this case the "big" money is in the 700 school districts (fiefdoms) across the state. Shouldn't we be aggressively seeking to consolidate and reduce non-instructional/administrative expenditures. Such real savings could be gained without losing a school's traditional identity/logo. We should at least institute the cap that was supposed to be part of the STAR program but due to politics was purged. Even our neighbors Massachusetts and New Jersey have caps on tax levies, 2.5% and 4% respectively. Conn. is moving to a 3% cap.

Summary:

- Even though there is considerable pressure to move to the income tax to finance Schools, like it or not property taxes are going to be a way of life in New York State for the foreseeable future.

- The New York State legislature must take rigorous, non-partisan action to transition the entire Real Property tax system out of the 20th century into the 21st century.

- A 21st century Real Property Tax system will include consolidating property assessments at the County level.

- The citizens of New York State need to demand that our legislators enact real cost reduction by consolidating non-instructional/administrative functions across our school districts.

- Local and County officials should work closely with our State officials in creating the 21st century Real Property Tax system and at the same time develop a pathway for assessing at the County level.

11. Access is the problem, not apathy. Change is past due.

February 19, 2008

Sup. Don Raw of the Canandaigua City School District wants to find out why people voted the way they did. I agree. I presume he is talking not only about those who voted YES (703) and those voting NO (904) but also those who did not vote (13,243). Let's focus on just one of the many issues, namely voter ACCESS.

The CCSD has a very large footprint, >20 miles NSEW, population >35,000. Yet there is only one voting booth in the schoolhouse on Pearl Street. There are probably more eligible voters than the 14,850 registered, making total non-voters greater than 13,243. A huge number which I hope and expect Mr. Raw and the Board are willing and anxious to take actions to see it reduced substantially.

Most non-CCSD workers are commuters spending 12-hour days at work and on the road. They do not have ACCESS to vote at their place of work. Need to determine turnout of this group.

All of the CCSD workers have ACCESS to vote at their place of work, as well as the choice of voting at different times during the day. Need to determine turnout of this group,

The CCSD continues to maintain an unfair and discriminatory voting system that suppresses the votes of non-CCSD workers due to lack of ACCESS and increases the votes of CCSD workers because they can vote in the schoolhouse, their place of work. This system is more suited to the last century than the 21st century. It's long past time for a change. To use an old term from last century let's start thinking, "out-side-the-box".

Conclusion: non-CCSD workers must have AC-CESS to voting near where they live.

CCSD workers also must have ACCESS to voting near where they live. Not at their place of work.

Sup. Raw's search for solutions should include;

- Set a modest goal for voter turnout, let's say 50% about 7,500 voters
- Work with General Election people to evaluate using some of their already established polling places throughout the District.

- Include absentee ballot forms in the "Digest" and with the tax bills themselves.

12. Fossil fuels are good, not evil

August 29, 2008

Environmental ideologues led by their high priest Al Gore are continuing to promote the myth of anthropogenic (human caused) global warming. They trumpet; "… the only way to save the planet is to stop using fossil fuels and reduce population growth". Their arguments have been proven to be replete with erroneous data and assumptions. We must resist the anti-fossil fuels environmentalists whose mission is to demonize, tax, and regulate them out of existence.

Let's put aside the apocalyptical rantings of the "global warming "crowd and discuss global unmet needs. World population is about 6.5 billion. There is a desperate need by billions of our neighbors for more food, shelter, clothing, water, medicines, energy, democracy, freedom, etc.… Global poverty is the crisis, not global warming.

Good old Mother Earth is like a garden, a cornucopia if you will of resources. Most individuals are responsible and creative gardeners of these riches. A continuous stream of goods for the betterment of humanity has resulted. This growing world productivity has improved the livelihoods of billions of people. Unfortunately, there are still billions who do not share in this harvest. We have a lot of work to do.

It's appropriate here to quote Pope John Paul II at a UN World Population Conference some years ago, he said, "The world doesn't need fewer people at the table but rather more bread on the table." With that challenge he has pointed the way.

When searching for solutions to a challenge it is always useful to identify success stories to similar challenges. A model if you will to learn from. Let's use the United States as an example of just such a success story.

The United States in just over 200 years has provided more freedom, more of the good life to more people both here at home and abroad than any other nation in history. Why such a glorious accomplishment?

We should begin in 1776 and speak of our Founding Fathers, their faith and vision, the Declaration of Independence, the Constitution. These and other related memorable events set our Nation, one Nation under God, on the right course for the future. Our example, the United States of America was founded on the basis of faith and freedom.

Let's pick up the story in the 19th century when America was moving toward 60 million, due largely to immigration. The first oil wells were being drilled. Production of coal and natural gas was on the increase. Inventions and developments, such as the electric light, internal combustion engine, farm equipment, railroads, automobiles, and the industrial revolution itself followed. Not far behind came the whole petrochemical industry with fertilizers, medicines, plastics and thousands of other products.

Yes, some 300 million of us now live in this Nation of freedom, opportunity and plenty and are thankful to those generations who have gone before for their hard work, creativity and sacrifices in war and peace, for achieving such accomplishments. We also must be thankful for the great resources of coal, oil and gas which provided the essential energy for this journey.

What the world needs now is more fossil fuel production, not less. Fossil fuels are 86% of the world's energy today and will continue to be the major source of the world's energy as we move through the

21st century. The US, over the last few decades has imperiled its economy and security by irresponsibly failing to use its own coal, oil and gas resources. The US must begin now to produce more of its own fossil fuel as well as all alternative sources of energy. In addition, more scientific research is needed to develop "new revolutionary energy" sources, yet unknown. It may very well be before the end of the 21st century the world will discover its "new energy" for the 22nd century and beyond.

13. Manmade global warming: scourge or scam

January 8, 2009

Over 30,000 scientists, including 9000 PhDs have signed a petition (www.petitionproject.com) extensively detailing why they believe the following:

"There is no convincing scientific evidence that human release of carbon dioxide, methane, or other greenhouse gases is causing or will, in the foreseeable future, cause catastrophic heating of the Earth's atmosphere and disruption of the Earth's climate. Moreover, there is substantial scientific evidence that increases in atmospheric carbon dioxide produce many beneficial effects upon the natural plant and animal environments of the Earth."

If after the reader has reviewed all the data in the "petition" signed on to by 30,000 scientists and is still an Al Gore believer, still is unconvinced, says more is needed to throw Al Gore overboard, read on.

US Senate EPW Committee's 231-page report of 12/11/08 states in its introduction, "Over 650 dissenting scientists from around the globe challenged man made global warming(MMGW) claims made by the United Nations Intergovernmental Panel on Climate Change(IPCC) and former VP Al Gore. These prominent international scientists include many current and former UNIPCC scientists who have turned against the UNIPCC." Let's listen to quotes from just a few of these prominent scientists:

"CO_2 emissions make absolutely no difference, one way or the other. Every scientist knows this, but it doesn't pay to say so."

"Global warming as a political vehicle keeps developing nations walking barefoot."

"I am convinced that the current alarm over carbon dioxide is mistaken... fears about MMGW are unwarranted and are not based on good science."

"Global warming scare mongering is being used as a political tool to increase government control over Americans lives, incomes and decision making."

"Warming fears are the worst scientific scandal in history. When people come to know what the truth is, they will feel deceived by science and scientists."

"So far real measurements give no ground for concern about a catastrophic future warming."

These two massive peer-reviewed scientific reports above should be more than enough to persuade the reader MMGW is a scam not a scourge.

Perhaps the most succinct quote re the subject of MMGW is the comment made by the new President of the European Union, Vaclav Klaus who says, "It has become a new religion or a new ideology…threatens to undermine freedom and the world's economic and social order."

The UN IPCC along with the Al Gore sycophants, including much of the MSM have wrongly propagandized catastrophic results for our planet if we humans don't stop producing energy from coal, oil and gas. These MMGW ideologues plan on putting the brakes on use of coal, oil and gas by making it so expensive nobody can afford to use energy generated from these sources. They propose various cap&trade, tax and punitive regulatory systems. (New York State already having by far the highest electric rates in the Nation, wrong-headedly began its own "Cap&trade" last year which will result in substantially higher energy costs for its citizens). They even propose an international legal system to place severe penalties on those countries, states that exceed allowable emissions standards. Standards set by the way by international emissions security organizations. All this ultimately to be orchestrated by that well known international organization, the United Nations. Well known that is for its unbelievable incompetence and corruption. Have no doubt about it powerful forces within the international, national and state governments are already developing legislation, forming the structures and networks to control, micromanage if you will, worldwide energy development and use. The arrogance of these MMGW ideologues is without precedent but never the less they have initiated this worldwide juggernaut to gather more power and money to themselves, to implement dangerous and costly solutions for false or unproven theoretical problems.

Our first President George Washington thought long and hard about the role of government. He said, "Government is not reason, it is not eloquent, it is force. Like fire it is a dangerous servant and a fearful master." It is clear this international, national and state governmental MMGW juggernaut is rapidly becoming our "fearful master ".

14. Know your enemy

April 5, 2009

Quote from "Art of War" by SUN TZU, Chinese General, 6th cent. BC; "If you know your enemies and know yourself you will not be imperiled in a hundred battles. If you do not know your enemies or yourself you will be imperiled in every single battle."

President Obama and his Administration are in the process of manipulating definitions surrounding the GWOT (Global war on terror) for example they have replaced GWOT with OCO (Overseas Contingency Operation). What is used if we have a domestic terrorist attack "Homeland Contingency Operation"? Sec. Napolitano, Homeland Security has removed the word "terrorist" and replaced it with "Man-made disaster". Has she has been charged with sexism because she didn't use "person-made disaster"? The term "enemy combatant" no longer can be used, not sure of replacement term. Most significantly the silence coming from the Obama team on the term "Islamist terrorist" is deafening. You just don't hear it.

Let's listen to the "The 9/11 Commission Report" (remember that) on page 362 describe the enemy.

"In this sense, 9/11 has taught us that terrorism against American interests "over there" should be regarded just as we regard terrorism against American interests "over here." In this same sense, the American homeland is the planet. But the enemy is not just 'terrorism.' Some generic evil. This vagueness blurs the strategy. The catastrophic threat at this moment in history is more specific. It is the threat posed by IS-LAMIST TERRORISM"—especially the Al Qaeda network, its affiliates and its ideology."

Also, page 47, Bin Ladin and Zawahiri issued a formal Declaration of War in the name of the "World Islamic Front" calling for the murder of any American, anywhere on earth and stating, "… it is the individual duty of every Muslim to do it in any country where it is possible to do it and not to differentiate between military and civilian targets."

More from the Report, "Bin Laden and Islamists terrorists mean exactly what they say: to them America is the font of all evil, the "head of the snake," and it must be converted or destroyed. It is not a position with which Americans can bargain or negotiate. With it there is no common ground-not even respecting life-on which to begin to dialogue. It can only be destroyed or utterly isolated."

Let's list just some of the horrendous atrocities the ISLAMIST TERRORISTS have committed against Americans starting with the first WTC bombing in 1993, Khobar Towers bombed 1996, US embassies in Kenya and Tanzania bombed in 1998, Battleship USS Cole bombed in 2000, and of course American Flight 11, crashing into the North Tower WTC at 8:47am, United Flight 175, crashing into the South Tower WTC at 9:03am, American Flight 77, crashing into the Pentagon at 9:37am, and United Flight 93, plowing into an empty field at 10:03am after heroic "Let's roll" actions by its passengers, all on that Tuesday morning September 11, 2001. These evil atrocities alone account for many thousands of dead, many more thousands of wounded and injured, a lifetime of grief for loving relatives, friends, fellow workers as well as enormous economic losses. As directed, the ISLAMIST TERRORISTS did not "differentiate between military and civilian targets". Many thousands more civilians were killed or wounded than military personnel.

Some of these individual ISLAMIST TERROR-ISTS, these enemy combatants, were captured, are being held at Gitmo. They have not only confessed to planning and carrying out the above atrocities but say they are proud of their acts and would do it again. President Obama has ordered Gitmo be closed and all prosecutions of these murderers be stopped. AG Holder says some will be released into the US, given legal help and aid to settle in our communities.

The 9/11 report defines our determined enemy in a thorough, specific, documented manner. It also describes who we were as a Nation on 9/12. Are we still that Nation?

Many thanks and gratitude to President Bush, his team and our military for their courageous actions and sacrifices over the years in protecting our Nation, preserving our freedoms and preventing any terrorist attacks on our Homeland since 9/11/01. However, as the time gap widens without an attack from a determined enemy, the odds of being attacked and with greater force shorten. Men and women in the military are still laying their lives on the line every day in this global war brought on by the Islamist terrorists and our thoughts and prayers are with them. As Churchill said re the RAF pilots during the Battle of Britain in 1940, "Never have so many owed so much to so few."

President Obama, his team and the military now under his command have that same, continuing awesome responsibility. Our support and prayers that they will be successful are with them. If there are any doubts or bewilderments by any members of the Obama team as to who the enemy is and that "they must be destroyed or utterly isolated", I would urge them to read "The 9/11 Commission Report".

15.   No CATT (Cap and Trade Tax)

May 8, 2009

A recent guest essayist said cap&trade legislation was needed to increase the cost to consumers of energy generated from coal, oil and gas and applauds Europe for having added "high gasoline taxes" and for having instituted a "cap&trade" regimen. These government-imposed regimens to solve MMGW have been an economic disaster for Europe, causing an explosion of energy costs with industry moving out due to failure to compete. By the way, currently, in New York State when you pay your utility bills >20% of total is taxes and >25% of your gasoline is taxes.

The essayist is conflicted. First, he urges cap&trade because to quote him, "it is the government setting prices for the common goods". In the very next paragraph he says, "Cap&trade gets the government out of the business of dictating solutions". Which is it? The national cap&trade regimen being promoted by Congressional leaders, Nancy Pelosi, Henry Waxman, Barbara Boxer and President Obama would result in a huge government bureaucracy and > $3,000 in increased energy costs for every man, woman and child in the nation. It is a very expensive, wrongheaded solution for a presumed problem with as yet no scientific consensus. The essay, with all due respect, is simply a re-hash of the same old tired, PC propaganda put out by Al Gore, the United Nations IPCC and their sycophants over the past several years.

I urge the reader to do his or her own research on the subject of MMGW and after you have made up your mind communicate your views (with a tea bag) to your reps in Washington. Some will say, "Oh I am too small to make a difference." Don't you believe it. Did you ever try to sleep with a mosquito in the room? I suggest going to www.petitionproject.com a peer-reviewed report by over 30,000 scientists (including over 9000 PhDs) who state, "there is no convincing scientific evidence that human release of carbon dioxide is causing or will in the foreseeable future cause catastrophic global warming", also refer to report by Senate Comm. On Environment and Public Works where over 700 dissenting scientists from around the globe challenge MMGW claims made by the United Nations IPCC and Al Gore. Check out the credentials of these eminent scientists many current and former IPCC scientists who have turned against the IPCC. These are only two of many highly credentialed sources available in 2009 to refute the "alarmists" of past years. Many members of Congress on both sides of the aisle are resisting the pressures of Pelosi, Waxman, Boxer and others to do "cap&trade". Some want to substitute a "simple nationwide tax" on carbon emissions in lieu of C&T. It would also be a foolish policy. Both of these regimens would impact about 75% of the nation's economy with literally millions of transactions being involved. Have any of these "alarmists" ever looked at the frigging nightmare of our current tax code.

The science behind global warming is not well understood and is far from settled. The number of dissenting climate scientists is greater by far than the number of climate scientists who contributed to the United Nations IPCC report. The number of highly qualified dissenters is far too large to ignore.

What should we do? I urge the reader to read article in NEWSWEEK, issue dtd 5/18/09. "The Bias Against Oil & Gas", by Robert J. Samuelson. The United States has hundreds of years of fossil fuels that can be used to generate our growing energy demands over the near term. The US must act now to produce more energy from our existing oil, coal, gas reserves and nuclear for the near term and many other alternatives such as solar, wind, geo-thermal and perhaps as yet unknown sources for the long term. We have to get the politicians out of road, abandon the false choices of C&T, energy taxes, government run energy systems and turn loose those basic American characteristics of hard work, creativity, technological & scientific advances, the will to see and seize economic opportunities and firm faith in the future that have always made this country the growing dynamic country that it is.

16. "Don't jump to any conclusions"

December 30, 2009

Nidal Malik Hasan, a Muslim, an Islamist terrorist, in a sneak attack on Nov. 5, 2009 killed 14, wounded over 30 defenseless soldiers at Fort Hood, Texas. Nidal shouted "Allah Akbar" as he was shooting his victims. President Obama cautioned, "Don't jump to any conclusions".

Abdulhakim Muhammad, a Muslim, an Islamist terrorist, in a sneak attack on June 1, 2009 shot 2 defenseless soldiers at a military recruiting station in Little Rock, Ark. Killing one and seriously wounding the other. Abdulhakim, showing no remorse, stated his atrocity was "...an act of God, for the sake of Allah, the Lord of the world". Common sense would say this was an act of Islamist terrorism but heeding the words of our President, "Don't jump to any conclusions".

Umar Farouk Abdulmutallab, a Muslim, an Islamist terrorist, in a sneak attack on Christmas Day set off a powerful explosive on board an airliner as it was descending to the Detroit airport. Fortunately, the device failed. Umar 's father weeks earlier warned the

U.S. Embassy in Nigeria that his son had traveled to Yemen and had become a dangerous religious fanatic. Obama's State Dept. did not revoke his visa, did not put him on a no-fly list. Apparently, Obama's State Dept. didn't want to "jump to any conclusions". President Obama, 3 days later referred to Umar as an "isolated extremist".

President Obama's words and actions are emboldening our enemies and disheartening our friends. Examples such as his flagellation of America in the Cairo Sermon, his refusal to support the freedom fighters in Iran, his cave in to enemy combatants and KSM for a show trial in NYC, endangering our heroic troops in Afghanistan with his PC rules of engagement, his attacks against the CIA, his censoring of the term "war on terror", as though by not seeing, speaking or hearing the term the global war on terror will go away, to name only a few. Common sense would indicate from these examples and others the President is coddling the enemy. But we shouldn't "jump to any conclusions".

The 9/11 Commission Report states, "…the enemy is not just 'terrorism', some generic evil. The catastrophic threat is more specific. It is the threat posed by ISLAMIST TERRORISM". It goes on, "…with it there is no common ground on which to dialogue. It can only be destroyed or utterly isolated".

The trend line of domestic attacks under President Obama in 2009 would indicate there will be more in 2010 unless Obama employs more aggressive strategies. First step must be to fire Janet Napolitano.

If President Obama and his team have any doubts or bewilderments about who the enemy is and what his goals are they need to read The 9/11 Commission Report. Surely, they have all read this report by now but we shouldn't "jump to any conclusions".

17. Remember 9/11, no mosque at ground zero

August 22, 2010

The bi-partisan "9/11 Commission Report" states the following…. "the enemy is not just 'terrorism,' some generic evil. The catastrophic threat is more specific. It is the threat posed by <u>ISLAMIST</u> terrorism. The enemy is sophisticated, patient, disciplined and lethal. The enemy rallies broad support in the Arab and Muslim world and its hostility toward us and our values is limitless. It makes no distinction between military and civilian targets. The Islamist terrorists mean exactly what they say: to them America is the font of all evil, the "head of the snake," and it must be converted or destroyed."

The report continues, "This is not a position with which Americans can bargain or negotiate. With it there is no common ground-not even respect for life-on which to begin a dialogue. It can only be destroyed or utterly isolated."

We are engaged in a global war brought on by acts of war by Islamist terrorists. These atrocities, included the first WTC (World Trade Center) bombing in

1993, U.S. embassies in Kenya and Tanzania in 1998, the destroyer USS Cole in 2000, the Nov. 2009 massacre of defenseless innocents at Fort Hood by the Muslim Hasan as he shouted "Allahu Akbar", resulted in the deaths of many and injuries to thousands, civilian and military. Space doesn't permit the listing of the many attacks around the world, on land, in the air, some successful (in the view of the Islamists) some deterred.

Four such acts of war tragically were not prevented and they were the horrendous atrocities on Tuesday morning, September 11, 2001. At 8:47am American Flight 11 crashed into the North Tower WTC, at 9:03am United Flight 175 crashed into the South Tower, at 9:37am Flight 77 crashed into the Pentagon, at 10:03am United Flight 93, after heroic "Let's roll" actions by its passengers, plowed into an empty field in Pennsylvania. These evil atrocities alone account for many thousands of dead, many more thousands of injured (still causing added early deaths today), a lifetime of grief for loving relatives, friends, fellow workers as well as enormous economic losses. As directed by their Muslim leaders, the Islamist terrorists, all

Muslims, acting in the name of Islam did not "differentiate between military and civilian targets".

The World Trade Center, the site of the most diabolical and deadly attack on American soil ever and which still contains remains of the victims, is now called Ground Zero and is truly hallowed ground. Those radical Muslims who are demanding a mosque be built at Ground Zero are not just being insensitive; they are clearly practicing a provocative form of Islamic triumphalism. They should listen to those moderate Muslims who urge tolerance and speak against such action.

The American people overwhelmingly oppose locating the mosque at Ground Zero. Unfortunately, there are some who believe in accommodation and appeasement of radical Muslims. It would be a good thing if these people would read the 9/11 Commission Report.

18. Back to basics - limited government

November 20, 2010

Well I have some good news and bad news. You all know the good news is the huge win across the country in the recent election. Republicans gained more than 650 seats in State legislatures, they control at least 55 chambers versus only 38 for the Democrats, now hold 30 Governorships and 243 or so House Congressional seats (gain of 64). Even New York State gained 6 House seats.

This big success was a vote for greater economic freedom & opportunity, lower debt, a smaller constitutionally based government, less taxes, less spending, individual freedom. It was a vote against Obamacare, Cap& Trade, stimulus and the greater centralization of government under the Obama-Pelosi-Reid troika. It was more than a vote, it was a restraining order!

It was a team effort; the candidates, Republicans, Independents, Tea Partiers, even some Democrats and all deserve a well done. By the way the Tea Partiers were the tip of the spear on this huge victory.

The bad news is that New York and Calif at the Governor and Senate levels decided to vote for "statuscuomo". We can talk about that later.

Reviewing this book, "The 5000 Year Leap", I read on page 5, "The answer to most of the problems is comparatively simple. Return to the fundamentals. Get back to the basics. Nothing in life is ever going to be perfect, but it can be much more gratifying and a lot less dangerous if we can get back to the fundamentals that provided that amazing 5,000-year leap in the first place."

David Barton, in "Original Intent" refers on pages 225 and 226 to the Bible being far and away the primary influence, inspiration on the Founders. Barton concludes, "The fact that the Founders quoted the Bible more frequently than any other source is indisputably a significant commentary on its importance in the foundation of our government. In fact, some have even conceded that 'historians are discovering that the Bible, perhaps even more than the Constitution, is our Founding document.'"

Going back to basics and first things. The Bible in the book of Genesis says, "…in His image He created him. Male and female He created them. Then God blessed them and said to the them, "Be fruitful and multiply; fill the earth and subdue it."

Pope John Paul II, "From the beginning therefore man is called to <u>work</u>. Work is one of the characteristics that distinguish man from the rest of the creatures. Man derives dignity from work, scientific, physical, cultural. <u>Work</u> is a fundamental dimension of man's existence."

Ben Franklin, "Idleness and pride tax with a heavier hand than kings and parliaments." Another of his quotes, "When the people find that they can vote themselves money, that will herald the end of the republic."

George Washington, "…of all the dispositions and habits which lead to political prosperity, religion and morality are indispensable supports." Another of his quotes, "It is the duty of all nations to acknowledge the providence of Almighty God, to obey His will, to be grateful for His benefits and humbly implore His protection and favors."

St. Augustine, "Pray as though everything depended upon God. <u>Work</u> as though everything depended upon you."

The Declaration of Independence states, "…all men are created equal, they are endowed by their Creator with certain unalienable Rights, that among these are Life, Liberty and the pursuit of Happiness." This God given Right to "pursue happiness" takes many forms but key is for the individual to securely and freely choose to expend his private labor(physical/intellectual), in conjunction with private capital/property (his or his associates) for the pursuit of his goals for happiness. Some will say there is an inherent contention between labor and capital and cite the many confrontations to back this claim. Others will cite the many cases of enlightened relationships that refute this claim. Actually, in a free entrepreneurial, capitalistic society as is America, they are necessary companions. Human <u>work</u> continuously produces human capital; together they draw on God's cornucopia of created riches for the betterment of mankind.

As the "5,000 year leap says, "It was in America that the founding Fathers assembled the 28 great ideas that produced the dynamic success formula, the Constitution, which proved such a sensational blessing to modern man"

During four long, hot summer months in Philadelphia in 1787 the founders worked tirelessly to create the main Constitution. After ratification by Congress it was sent to the states for ratification with their amendments. There were many. James Madison was key in reducing these to ten (the now famous Bill of Rights). They were finally approved in 1791. It is the 10th amendment that addresses "Limited Government" as follows: "The powers not delegated to the United States by the Constitution nor prohibited by it to the states, are reserved to the states respectively, or to the people." Thus was created the Constitutional Republic with political equilibrium between the people in the states and the federal government. Keeping the power base close to the people, strong local self-government and with a federal government of limited defined powers.

As Patrick Henry said, "The Constitution is not an instrument to restrain the people; it is an instrument to restrain the government."

As we enter the 21st century this governmental "equilibrium" has continuously and tragically become unbalanced. We are now truly far adrift from our founding principles and constitutional limits. To quote Newt Gingrich, "This Obama-Pelosi-Reid system is clearly a secular-socialist machine and Obama is the most radical President in American history"

The history of the world is replete with failed totalitarian societies such as those of communist states who collectivize the means of production, confiscate lands and farms, suppress religion, economic and political freedoms and in effect set themselves up as a kind of alternative god. The list is long of those who, quoting Ronald Reagan, have "ended up in the dust bins of history". Quoting Reagan again, "Freedom is never more than one generation away from extinction. We didn't pass it to our children in our bloodstream. It must be fought for, protected and handed on for them to do the same, or one day we will spend our sunset years telling our children and our children's children what it was once like in the United States where men were free."

There are many issues that need fixing. This will not happen easily or overnight. They all will require a grassroots movement that puts strong and sustained pressure on 545 people. Excerpts from column by Charley Reese (1980's), "100 Senators, 435 Congressmen, one President and nine Supreme Court jus-

tices. In this Nation of over 300 million these 545
human beings are directly, legally, morally and indi-
vidually responsible for the current state of America
and these 545 people are the ones who are responsible
for fixing it, with the 24/7, hard work, education, and
follow-up brought to them by the people.

There are no insoluble government problems. Do
not let these 545 people shift the blame to bureau-
crats, whom they hire and whose jobs they can abol-
ish; to lobbyists, whose gifts and advice they can reject; to regulators, to whom they give the power to
regulate and from whom they can take it.

Above all, do not let them con you into the belief
that there exist disembodied mystical forces like the
"economy," "inflation" or "politics" that prevent
them from doing what they take an oath to do.

Those 545 people and they alone are responsible.
They and they alone have the power. They and they
alone should be held accountable by the people who
are their bosses- provided they have the gumption to
manage their own employees."

The recent election was an outstanding example
of the people "managing their employees" Many of
the incumbent 545 were "fired". It will be necessary

to fire & replace many more in the near future to restore America. We will be judged by how well we do our job by our children and grandchildren.

19. Roberts Rules of Disorder

July 4, 2012

We now have Robert's Rules of Disorder, otherwise known as Obamacare, being declared constitutional.

The recent decision by Chief Justice Roberts to re-write the legislation in order to declare it constitutional as a tax was akin to making a constitutional silk purse out of an unconstitutional sow's ear.

Listen to Justices Kennedy, Thomas, Alito, Scalia on their powerful dissent,... "We cannot re-write the statute to be what it is not...Robert's decision is not a tax for the Anti-Injunction Act but it is a tax for constitutional purposes, that carries verbal wizardry too far, deep into the forbidden land of sophistry."

All that was wrong with Obamacare is still wrong, but tragically it now is the law of the land. Much has been written, talked about regarding the very wrong-headed bad legislative and regulatory detail. Obamacare is a monstrosity, opening the gates wide to a socialistic America and elimination of its citizen's constitutional freedoms. Suffice it to say it is the octopus of big government, centralized coercive power, higher taxes, greater regulation, health care of lesser quality and higher costs.

Repeal of Obamacare in totality is critical. It will only be achieved by a huge win at the ballot box in November 2012 by those who support repeal. The election in November 2010 was a huge win brought on chiefly by those outraged by passage of Obamacare in 2010.

Now citizens must work to identify those who support repeal of Obamacare and those who defend it.

We could refer to them as REPEALERS and DEFENDERS. Once the citizens have determined those candidates who are ROs (Repealers of Obamacare) and those who are DOs (Defenders of Obamacare) they need to work for and ultimately vote for those who support their position.

New York State has one state wide Senatorial and several regional Congressional races in progress right now. Find out which candidate is an RO and which is a DO. Call on the candidate personally, insist the candidate give specifics as to their position. Make them give straight answers. Speak out at their town meetings. It is a critical time for all patriots to step up to the plate. This is not the time for indifference. No time for citizens to say "Let George do it". He died over 200 years ago. It's up to you. We have less than four months to work to take our country back in November.

20. NYS scandalous abortion industry & Governor Cuomo

January 10, 2013

Governor Cuomo, otherwise known as the Abortion Governor of the state with the highest abortion rate at 38% of pregnancies, double the national average, far in excess of number two, California at 28%. Cuomo in his 2 years as Governor has presided over the violent killing of more than 300,000 babies or 600 innocent, defenseless brothers and sisters for every regular work day. Yes, New York State, the Empire State is No. 1; it truly is the abortion Capital of the nation.

Governor Cuomo in his State of the State continues to call for passage of the Reproductive Health Act. He says passage will provide greater access to those seeking abortion. He says NYS can do better because after all "It is her body". This despite reams of scientific/medical proof that from conception onward pregnancy involves 2 or more separate bodies. This despite a Dec. 2012 Marist poll saying 83% of Americans urge significantly greater abortion restrictions.

The Reproductive Health Act (RHA) declares abortion a "fundamental reproductive right". To name only a few objections. It would provide full legal cover to the tragic practice of abortion-on-demand through all nine months pregnancy. It would prohibit even basic and widely supported protection such as parental consent. It prevents any limits on taxpayer funded abortions. It places conscience protection for hospitals, medical professionals and other health providers in serious jeopardy.

Governor Cuomo, the abortion Governor is clearly following in the extreme pro-abortion footsteps of President Obama, our abortion President. They are truly waging a tyrannical war on the right to life of the unborn.

Thomas Jefferson says, "All tyranny needs to gain a foothold is for people of good conscience to remain silent." The people of New York State need to speak out and act to defeat the Reproductive Health Act.

21. No Catholic should belong to the Democrat party

July 2, 2013

Political parties over the life of our nation have held differing and evolving agendas. Now in the early part of the 21st century the Democrat party stands for and is committed to a secular, collectivist form of government with rights and values determined by, and flowing to the people from, a centralized state power. Its entire big government, high taxes, socialistic philosophy is the antithesis of the principle of subsidiarity of which Pope John Paul II spoke in strong support in his 1991 encyclical Centesimus Annus. Essentially this principle holds that nothing should be done by a large, complex organization which can be done by a smaller, simpler organization.

There are many examples of the Democrat party's big government approach. Their latest abomination is the passage of Obamacare. This grab for centralized power is attempting to collect 1/5 of our nation's economy under the control of 15 appointed members of the Independent Payment Advisory Board (IPAB) with coercive powers being given to 16,000 new IRS agents. This law, not only violates the principles of subsidiarity, but among many other things within its regulations, strips out protections for the unborn and religious liberty.

The USCCB has pronounced again, the Year of Faith 2013 with three primary goals, protect the unborn, marriage and religious liberty. The USCCB states, "...political forces are injecting themselves into the lives of Catholics and Church organizations, substituting their own secular theology for the Church's beliefs." The Bishops call forcefully for prayers and actions because the unborn, marriage and religious liberty are under assault as never before.

Speaking as a Catholic, former Democrat, and a firm believer in the Year of Faith, I urge Catholics to do three things. First for those Catholics who may be registered as Democrats opt out of the Democrat party. Second re-register as either a no-party-registrant or to a party more compatible with your beliefs. This "opting out" of the Democrat party would include Catholic Church leaders, both clergy and lay, who might still be registered Democrats. No-party-registrants will be unable to vote in party primaries but there are many other ways to impact the political process. Third, for the Year of Faith 2013 and beyond, do as St. Augustine said, "Pray as though everything depended on God. Work as though everything depended upon you."

❖

22. Christians should opt out of the democrat party

January 19, 2014

Governor Andrew Cuomo, the Democrat Governor of New York State pronounces, "Extreme conservatives (defined by the Gov. as those who support protection of the unborn, traditional marriage and the 2nd amendment) have no place in the state of New York."

Political parties over the life of our Nation have held differing and evolving agendas. Now in the early part of the 21st century the Democrat party, under the leadership of President Obama and his Democrat team members such as Leaders Reid & Pelosi, NY's Gov. Cuomo, etc., stands for and is committed to a secular, socialist form of big government with rights and values determined by, and flowing to the people from a centralized power. President Obama claims "America is not a Christian nation". Much historical documentation refutes this claim, see David Barton's excellent book "Original Intent" as just one example. Christianity, of course, is the religion that shaped America and made her what she is today.

The Democrat party's collectivist ideology is the antithesis of the Nation's founding constitutional principles. Its unrelenting attacks against the unborn, traditional marriage and religious liberty among other issues confirm its secular agenda.

Let's say a few words in support of the unborn, the most innocent and defenseless of our brothers and sisters right here in New York State, as January 22, is the 41st anniversary of Roe vs Wade. NYS under Gov. Cuomo and his Democrat team is known as the abortion capital of the Nation. Now in the 21st century scientific and medical knowledge about the unborn is far greater than back in the last century. Science has established the unborn feels pain at 20weeks fetal age.

Ten states (others to follow) have passed laws banning abortions of babies at 20 weeks fetal age. The House of Representatives passed H. R. 1797-Pain Capable Unborn Child Protection Act last year with 222 Republicans voting in support of protection for the unborn and 190 Democrats opposed to such protection including Leader Pelosi's NO vote. Of New York state Democrats voting, all 21 (100%) agreed with Leader Pelosi and voted against protecting the unborn. King Cuomo grants these 21 his permission to stay in NYS. A companion bill S-946 has been introduced in the Senate for action this year. Nationwide polls show that 64% of the people support such protection for the unborn.

Speaking as a Christian, a former Democrat and a firm believer in our Constitutional principles, no Christian should belong to today's Democrat party. The options would be to opt out if a registered Democrat, register with no-party affiliation or register with a party more compatible with your beliefs.

23. Pollyannaism run amuck

April 21, 2014

A columnist in his recent essay urges the nation to "move on with Obamacare" and "not to cry over spilt milk". Reading his essay reminded me of that wonderful 20th century novel "Pollyanna" wherein the main character Pollyanna was optimistic about events no matter the circumstances. This columnist clearly believes Obamacare is "spilt milk" otherwise he wouldn't be telling us not to cry over it. He is following the lead of many Democrats who are frantically ducking and dodging the issue, saying the nation has other priorities, it will work out eventually, don't have time to talk about it, etc...

Actually, Obamacare is not just "spilt milk" it is a train wreck, as some of its original creators now belatedly admit. The nation doesn't have time to cry over it because it is about the business of repealing it. Some say "let's just fix Obamacare". Impossible. When a car is a wreck beyond fixing it is declared "totaled" and sent to that graveyard of all wrecks, the crusher.

Space and time doesn't permit the list of scandalous, lying tactics by President Obama, Democrat leaders Pelosi and Reid, other Democrats to get the 2700-page Obamacare bill passed/signed. All will remember Democrat Leader Pelosi declaring "we'll find out what's in it after we pass it", President Obama and other Democrats with lying promises of, "You can keep your Doctor, you can keep your policy, it will reduce your cost by 2,500 dollars". Obamacare now has over 20,000 pages of regulations, orchestrated by the outrageously, incompetent, lying Kathleen Sebelius, and enforced by thousands of new IRS agents. President Obama, in order to attempt to avert a Democrat political disaster this coming November has unconstitutionally, deferred, waived, changed large parts of the law passed by the Democrats in Congress and signed by him during a gala, public signing ceremony.

Actually, Chief Justice Roberts changed (violation of the Constitution Art I, Sect. 1) the Obamacare legislation as signed into law by calling the penalty a tax, thereby allowing him erroneously to declare the individual mandate constitutional. A number of lawsuits are working their way thru the courts charging Obamacare is in violation of the Constitution's Origination Clause Art. I, Sec. 7. In addition to other lawsuits, the SCOTUS has heard and will rule in June on Obamacare being in violation of the first freedom in the first Amendment, the guarantee of religious freedom.

The fact is Obamacare is too big to succeed and is the antithesis of the nation's constitutional principles such as limited government and individual freedom. Because Democrat Senate Leader Reid has continuously blocked the Senate from voting on House passed bills calling for repeal, it is essential to elect enough Senators supporting repeal this November for Congress to pass and place the Obamacare repeal bill on President Obama's desk for signature early in the 114th Congress. If President Obama vetoes this bill, as expected, it will be up to Congress, in which all legislative powers have been vested (see Art. I sec. 1) to carry out the will of the people and override his veto.

❖

24. Benghazi; Islamist terrorist attacks 9/11/2012, so many questions, so few answers

June 5, 2014

The 9/11 Benghazi atrocity landscape, before, during and after the Islamist terrorist attacks is strewn with dereliction of duty events, raising "high Crimes and Misdemeanors" on the near horizon. See Art. II, Sec.4. The Benghazi plate is not the only dereliction of duty plate being served up by President Obama and his Administration. There are many more. To name only a few, the IRS, unconstitutional Executive Orders, attacks on religious liberty and freedom of the press, Fast & Furious, Veteran Health Care debacles, surrender of the "Gitmo Top 5 Islamist terrorists", refusal "to take Care that the Laws be faithfully executed". See Art. II, Sec.3, etc...

BEFORE 9/11 ISLAMIST TERRORIST AT-TACKS- President Obama, exceeding his constitutional authority, without congressional permission, ordered the U. S. military to "piggy-back," on the British and French in their military support in Libya of the Rebels against Qaddafi. Qaddafi was killed in

Nov. 2011. Libya has not had a functioning government structure since. Different parts of the country
are run by competing anti-Qaddafi (Islamist) re-
bels/militias. Obama sent Ambassador Stevens and a
few CIA agents into Benghazi, in the middle of this
quagmire to set up a make-shift consulate with a CIA
annex. The Int'l Red Cross office closed up and
moved out after being hit by RPGs in May 2012. In
June RPGs hit the British Ambassador's convoy,
causing the Brits to close their consulate. Ambassador
Stevens in the months preceding 9/11 because of the
deteriorating, violent conditions, repeatedly asked the
State Dept for more security. Each and every request
for more security was refused by the State Dept. In
fact, the State Dept. removed what little security exist-
ed in late August.

DURING 9/11 ISLAMIST TERRORIST AT-
TACKS- At 3:40 pm Wash. time the 1st attack began.
Ambassador Stevens immediately called Deputy Chief
Greg Hicks in the Tripoli Embassy and just before the
line went dead said, "Greg, we're under attack". Hicks
told all agency heads by 4pm Wash. time, including
the White House and State Dept., "Benghazi is under
a terrorist attack". Hicks was aware of huge military

bases and the 6th fleet within minutes flight time. Hicks told the defenders in Benghazi, fight on, help will be coming. Help never came. The battle raged on, Ambassador Stevens and Sean Smith were killed. All consulate personnel, under severe attack by upwards of 100 Islamist terrorists, abandoned the consulate and retreated to the CIA annex, a better defensive position. During this time Ansar al-Shariah (affiliate of al-Qaeda) twittered their claim of credit for the attack.

Back in Washington, President Obama spoke with Sec. of Defense Panetta and CJCS Gen. Dempsey at 5pm. Pres. Obama spoke with Sec. of State Clinton at 10pm. Sec. Clinton shortly afterward stated the Benghazi "demonstration" caused by "inflammatory material posted on the internet" (you tube video). President Obama and Sec. Clinton, though they had no idea how long these attacks would continue or if they might very well expand to Tripoli, chose not to even try to defend their embattled fellow Americans. They chose to abandon them on the battlefield.

Back in Benghazi, now about midnight Wash, time (6am 9/12/12 Benghazi time), Tyrone Woods, Glenn Doherty and a few others were under attack by RPG, mortar and machine gun fire. Woods and

Doherty were soon killed by mortar fire, just hours after Sec. Clinton had announced, this "demonstration" was caused by a video. The Americans fighting for their very lives on the ground in Benghazi knew this was a planned, organized, heavily armed Islamist terrorist attack and in no way was a "street demonstration" by a handful of protestors.

AFTER 9/11 ISLAMIST TERRORIST ATTACKS- Because President Obama and his Administration continue to stonewall, dissemble and obstruct, it was necessary to create the new House Select Committee on Benghazi. Its purpose under Chairman Trey Gowdy is to finally get all the facts, the whole truth on what has been called the most egregious cover-up in history.

25. Checks and balances and President Obama

August 8, 2014

James Madison, our 4th President, one of the principle architects of the U. S. Constitution, was a strong advocate that it include "checks and balances" between the Legislative, Executive and Judicial branches. Such rules, under the Constitutional Republic framework of separation of powers, allow one branch to limit another. Just two of many examples of these rules are: First, the Legislative branch, House of Representatives, "...shall have the sole Power of Impeachment" (see Art. I Sec. 2). Second, every bill passed by the Legislative branch, "...shall be presented to the President of the United States; and before the Same shall take Effect, shall be approved by him..." (see Art. 1 Sec. 7). The President has the authority to reject/veto Legislative bills.

Madison's famous quote in Federalist 51, "...if men were angels, no government would be necessary" captures his reasoning. Madison believed "checks and balances" rules were necessary to help limit government and its abuses and to protect citizen's liberty and individual rights.

The truthful, documented, voluminous record of President Obama's lawless actions/inactions, in violation of his constitutional authority provide overwhelming justification for his impeachment. The subject of impeachment and the reasons for it absolutely should not be taken off the table. This very important political debate between those who support President Obama's agenda "to transform America" and those who support the principles/framework of our Constitutional Republic not only needs to be continued but intensified. This, as an integral part of education for "we the people".

As James Madison has said, "A well-instructed people alone can be permanently a free people."

President Obama is confident his base, which includes the MSM, crony- capitalists, academia, Saul Alinsky zealots, extreme environmentalists, etc., a formidable army, will turn out and vote on Election Day November 4th for his team.

The 2 goals of patriots who support limited government, individual freedom, the principles and framework of our Constitutional Republic are as follows: First, to achieve a maximum voter turnout on Election Day November 4th (less than 3 months away). Second, to win a majority of like-minded candidates to be seated in the 114th Congress, both House and Senate. Only by doing this can we begin early-on to curtail/block President Obama's impeachable transgressions and begin to move America in the right direction. If after these wins, he and his acolytes still are inviting impeachment (doubtful), and the nation's political winds are in support, I say let's make their day!

26. Presidential leadership

September 4, 2014

America is engaged in a global war brought on by Islamic Supremacism, conducted by Islamist terrorists, their networks, their affiliates and their ideology. They are united in their belief the enemy is the West and it must be conquered. Conquered means the people of the West have three choices, convert to Islam, pay an onerous tax to stay alive as a 3rd class subject or be killed. Their atrocities against apostates, mainly Christians and Jews, are too many and too horrific to list here but they have forced non-Muslims to flee by the hundreds of thousands from lands they have lived in for generations.

President Obama has failed to lead America in this war. He refuses to use the term Islamic, Muslim in defining our enemy and orders his team to do likewise. One of his first acts upon becoming President was to change the term "Global War on Terror" to "Overseas Contingency Operation". There are many examples of President Obama re-defining reality. Just to name a few, all federal training manuals for law enforcement and intelligent agents including FBI agents have been purged of the terms Islam and Jihad, Benghazi talking points were purged of these terms and the now infamous video excuse was substituted, Fort Hood atrocity where Major Hasan (card carrying Soldier of Allah) shot 45 people killing 14 shouting "Allahu Akbar" was and still is called "workplace violence", although all knew immediately the Boston Marathon bombing was an act of terror he initially refused to call it that and said "let's not jump to conclusions". During Obama's Presidency there have been 21 Islamist Terrorists Attacks on U. S. soil from 2008 thru June 2014, killing 46 and injuring 300.

President Obama's discordant rhetoric and bizarre actions confuse and mis-lead the public as to who the enemy is and its evil, existential threat. One can only hope that our President soon begins to tell it like it is and act accordingly.

Let's take a brief look at two great Presidential leaders:

President F. D. Roosevelt during election year 1940, in spite of huge opposition completed the "Destroyer Deal" with Great Britain and instituted the military draft. He spoke to Congress on Dec. 8, 1941 calling "Dec. 7, 1941 a day of infamy", 33 minutes later Congress voted a Declaration of War on Japan. In large part due to FDR's leadership the world survived the evil onslaughts of the Axis powers and today's Americans, most of whom were not yet born, are eternally grateful for his Presidential leadership.

President R. Reagan's theory of the cold war was, "We win they lose". In a 1982 speech to the British Parliament, "...the forward march of freedom and democracy will leave Marxism-Leninism on the ashheap-of-history." In 1983 the famous "Evil Empire" speech, "They preach to supremacy of the state, declare its omnipotence over individual man and predict its eventual domination over all peoples of the earth. They are the focus of evil in the modern world." In 1987 at the Bradenburg Gate near the Berlin Wall he challenged, "Mr. Gorbachev tear down this wall". The wall came down in 1989. In large part due to President Reagan's leadership the Evil Empire of Godless Communism (Reagan's words) was defeated and today's Americans, many of whom were not yet born are eternally grateful for his Presidential leadership.

There are other examples down thru history of Presidents who have been great leaders during times of crisis when it is necessary "to provide for the common defense." Now is a time of crisis, where is the nation's leader?

27. Earthquake election win for republicans on November 4, 2014

Rev. December 30, 2014

The recent earthquake election win across the nation for Republicans resulted in the following numbers by party being seated in the 114th US Congress beginning Jan. 6, 2015, State Governors and State Legislatures.

	Repub.	Demo.	Ind/na.	Ttl.
US Senate	54	44	2	100
US House	247	188	0	435
State Governors	31	18	1	50
State Legislatures	68	30	1	99

This unprecedented win by the Republican candidates with the votes of not only Republicans but also Democrats and Independents is a wakeup call from "we the people" who want to change President Obama's and his team's goals to "transform America", to the goals compatible with the principles of our Constitutional Republic.

The 114th Congress begins on Tuesday, January 6, 2015 and must, with a high degree of urgency, take up its responsibilities as specified in the Constitution, "...with a firm reliance on the protection of divine Providence." First under Art. I, Sec. 1 "All legislative Powers herein granted shall be vested in the Congress of the United States". The 114th Congress must begin to take back those Executive decrees, absent Executive authority earlier congresses ceded to the Executive branch. This Congress must pass bills on issues that were winning issues during their election campaigns. Of course, the President under the Constitution has the authority to veto each and every one of them. Presidential vetoed bills are returned to the Senate for a sustaining or over-ride vote.

Let's take just two critical issues that were major reasons for the Republicans winning, Repeal Obamacare and the Keystone pipeline. The 114th Congress should on day one send a Repeal Obamacare bill to the President, in addition many bills repealing specific requirements in Obamacare such as the medical device tax, IPAB (Independent Payment Advisory board), individual mandates, to name only a few. President Obama will certainly wear out his pen vetoing some or all of these bills but it will be up to the sitting Senators be they Democrat, Republican or Independent to support or over-ride the President's veto. Just remember half (30) the Senators (all Demos) who voted for Obamacare will be gone in 2015. Let the record show how each Senator voted on the many destructive issues and "abuses and usurpations" of Obamacare.

The 114th Congress should on day one pass and send the Keystone Pipeline bill to the President. This would be the "keystone" of many energy related bills to take advantage of our nation's largest coal, oil and natural gas reserves in the world. This would improve the economy and initiate more jobs. The President can approve and sign it or veto and return it to the Senate for a sustaining or over-ride vote.

The 114th Congress, under Leaders Boehner and McConnell, early and sustained legislative actions resulting from listening to the re-awakening call of the people in Nov. will determine not only the success of the 114th Congress but Presidential elections in 2016.

A word of warning to all members of the 114th Congress, stop acting like those sailors in Greek mythology who listened to the siren calls of the mermaids on their rocky beach and stop listening to the siren calls of special interest, moneyed, lobbyists. Wake up 114th Congress, the people have spoken.

28. New York State again votes to protect the unborn

January 16, 2015

The recent AP article about the New York State Senate Republican majority once again not passing Governor Cuomo's pro-abortion bill quoted NYS Senator Stewart-Cousins, Westchester Democrat Leader as being highly critical of her Republican Senate colleagues for their vote to protect the unborn.

In the interest of being fair and balanced (the AP article was not) Lori Kehoe, New York State Right to Life Executive Director states, "How many times do New Yorkers have to reject the radical agenda that would legalize abortion for any reason through all 9 months. New York is already the abortion capital of the world, with no practical oversight of its abortion industry." Governor Cuomo in supporting passage of his bill says, "NYS can do better, after all it's her body". This, despite medical & scientific facts that from conception onward pregnancy involves two or more separate bodies. By doing better he not only means abortion-on-demand through 9 months but also removing conscience protections for hospitals, medical professionals and other health care providers. Governor Cuomo in his 4 years as Governor has presided over the killing of more than 500,000 babies, our innocent, defenseless sisters and brothers.

42 years after Roe v Wade (Jan 22, 1973) in this year 2015 we have monumentally greater knowledge about the baby in the womb than was known in the last century in the year 1973. We can now watch the baby during its gestation period through advances in Ultra Sound and other techniques. Remarkable advances in fetal surgery and other medical interventions are achieving truly miraculous results. Many medical professionals urge the use of fetal anesthesia because the fetus/baby experiences pain as early as 11 weeks. As this greater medical & scientific knowledge and the people's "good conscience" about the pre-born has progressed so also has state & federal legislation for the protection of this rapidly growing baby. One of many such bills is H. R. 36 Pain-Capable Unborn Child Protection Act just introduced Jan. 6, 2015 in the new 114th Congress. The House Republican majority is expected to vote and pass it on January 22, 2015, the same day as the March for Life in Washington and the42nd anniversary of Roe v Wade. The bill

will be sent to the Senate for passage and from there to President Obama for his signature or veto.

Governor Cuomo, the Abortion Governor, is following in the extreme pro-abortion footsteps of our Abortion President, President Obama. They are truly waging a tyrannical war on the right to life of the unborn and it must end.

29. Netanyahu tells it like it is

March 4, 2015

Prime Minister Netanyahu's historical speech Mar. 3rd in Congress was outstanding. He identified the enemy waging global war on political and religious freedoms of apostates be they Jews, Christians, Muslims, others as Militant Islam. He placed ISIS and IRAN as two major players in that group whose announced goals are the elimination of America and Israel. These two major players are competing for the crown of Militant Islam. If ISIS is defeated and IRAN gets nuclear weapons we have won the battle and lost the war. He says in this case, "The enemy of my enemy is my enemy".

The Prime Minister spoke with more clarity and substance on the issues than any American politician in recent years. He spoke candidly, boldly and informatively not only of the enemy confronting the free world but also on the "deal" President Obama is now negotiating with IRAN to prevent them from producing nuclear weapons. PM Netanyahu, in effect, conducted an invaluable seminar on the threats to the world, to the security of America and to the very survival of Israel of an IRAN with nuclear weapons. His audience was not only the packed house (he rec'd many standing ovations) but to millions around the world. The PM's discourse was an educational tour de force because of its worldwide audience, its timing and the insight and heartfelt truthfulness of the speaker himself.

The Prime Minister in reference to the "deal" was clear he believed, "No deal is better than a bad deal". He is convinced that a better deal can and should be negotiated. Such a better deal would not have a sunset time, would have IRAN stop aggression on its neighbors, stop sponsoring global terrorism and stop proclaiming the annihilation of Israel. It would also not leave IRAN's nuclear weapons production infrastructure intact and curtail the production of ICBMs. Most important it would strengthen the "trust and verify" aspects of the entire agreement. If IRAN refuses a better deal than more and stronger sanctions should be exacted. He was absolutely firm in his belief that IRAN must not have nuclear weapons. Not only would it instigate a rush by neighboring countries to acquire nuclear weapons but it would be an existential threat to Israel and Israel would be obligated to defend itself, hopefully with the assistance of its long-time ally America.

There are many examples of courageous leaders through history who have "told it like it is" in times of national or world crisis.

One such example is Patrick Henry in March 1775, exactly 240 years ago when he said, "...we are apt to shut our eyes against a painful truth. Are we disposed to be of the number of those having eyes, see not, having ears, hear not? We are told we are weak. There is a just God who presides over the destinies of nations. Is life so dear or peace so sweet, as to be purchased at the price of chains and slavery! I know not what others may take, but as for me, give me liberty or give me death!"

Another such example is Winston Churchill, "Still if you will not fight for the right when you can easily win without bloodshed, if you will not fight when your victory will be sure and not too costly, you may come to the moment when you will have to fight with all the odds against you and only a precarious chance of survival. There may even be a worse case you may have to fight when there is no hope of victory, because it is better to perish than live as slaves."

Two questions. Where are the nations of the Middle East, Africa, & Europe on WC's scale? Where is the good old USofA?

30. Man, woman, marriage, SCOTUS

June 15, 2015

When all else fails it is time to rely on the truth, the fundamentals. Men and women were created both different and complementary to each other. Their biological/physical structures are different but complementary. The characteristics of femininity and of masculinity are different but complementary. To deny this truth is to deny human nature and the purpose of life. Yes, men and women are different and since their beginning, both men and women, have said, "Thank God for the difference". Just listen to the words of that great song, "As Time Goes By", "...a woman needs a man, a man must have his mate, on that you can rely. It's still the same old story, the fundamental things apply... "

Marriage is a lifelong, committed, loving relationship between one man and one woman. The term marriage stands alone. Adding adjectives to the term marriage such as gay, same-sex, polygamous, polyandrous, etc. does not change the true nature of marriage. If the relationship between various individuals is other than the one above, it can be called a civil union, legal contract or something else but it is not marriage. These other legal relationships can reasonably resolve unfair, irrational, bizarre tax laws and other needs rightfully demanded by same-sex couples and others. In the interest of fairness what needs to be changed/eliminated are those unfair, irrational, bizarre governmental regulations, not the definition of marriage.

Marriage is a monogamous, faithful, heterosexual (man/woman) institution that has been the keystone of civilizations for multiple millennia. Support for it comes from respect for the natural law. Its essential purpose is procreation and responsible child rearing. Societies, the people, over the millennia have taken a strong and protective position to protect the institution of marriage because the well-being and strength of the institution of marriage and family is critical to the well-being and strength of the society and the people. We the people must continue to protect marriage.

The SCOTUS now in the 21st century, after years of substituting politics for constitutional law has perhaps become the most dangerous of our branches of government. It is a growing threat to the constitutional principle of participatory self-government. With its 9 unelected, lifetime appointed justices and its unconstitutional, aggressive overreach; it has become, in effect, the final word on questions of constitutionality. Some even refer to SCOTUS as a "national theology board". These 9 justices, and perhaps as few as 5 do not have the constitutional authority to redefine marriage and hence the institution of marriage. Yet again on Friday, June 26, the Court by a 5-4 vote chose to make another unconstitutional political decision and declare all 50 states must allow same-sex marriage. As I recall the Constitution of the United States begins, "We the People of the United States, in Order to form a more perfect Union…" Not "We the SCOTUS in order to dictate to the people, etc.."

31. Drawing and Quartering in the 21ˢᵗ Century

July 22, 2015

The horrific news of Planned Parenthood harvesting hearts, lungs, livers and other organs of the unborn for sale is remindful of the practice in centuries past of punishing those guilty of treason by "drawing and quartering". No need to describe the barbaric detail but the victim was deemed to be guilty and there is no record of the victim's severed body parts being put up for sale. In Planned Parenthood's case of course, the victim is innocent and its body parts, very carefully severed to insure their marketability, are put up for sale. How did this "slaughter of the innocents" in the "land of the free and the home of the brave" come to be?

The SCOTUS, made up of nine unelected, lifetime appointed Justices; in the last century (1973) Roe v Wade decision used raw judicial power to decide a right to abortion. A right that is nowhere to be found in the text of the constitution. This last century Supreme Court decision is now infamous for many reasons. First, since 1973 it has sentenced over 55 million babies to death by techniques even more barbaric than "drawing and quartering". Second, those 7 Justices who voted yes did not have the scientific and medical knowledge at that time in the last century that is now available in this century in the year 2015. Through their ignorance, arrogance and willingness to politicize the issue those 7 Justices are directly responsible for this "slaughter of the innocents". Those 7 Justices were all born between 1898 and 1915, 100 years ago, 4 or 5 generations in the past. Each of those justices had a right to life in their Mother's womb, yet in the middle of the last century they chose to strip away that right for the unborn. Those 7 Justices all died in the last century leaving an unbelievable bloody and unjust legacy.

Now in the 21st century thru Ultra-Sound we can see the baby in the womb, we know the baby experiences pain at 20 weeks gestation and even earlier. Because of many 21st century scientific/medical breakthroughs truly miraculous medical interventions are accomplished such as fetal surgery. Unfortunately, Planned Parenthood uses these modern medical techniques to harvest the unborn's organs for sale.

Progress is being made to protect the unborn. The Pain Capable Unborn Child Protection Act H. R. 36 was passed by the House with 242 yes and 184 no votes. Yes votes included 238 Republicans, no votes included 180 Democrats. The companion bill in the Senate is S-1553. It will be voted on in a few weeks, passed, sent to President Obama who has promised to veto it. Congress will than have an up or down vote to override his veto. In the meantime, we the people have to urge our politicians in office or running for office at the State or Federal level to protect the unborn.

32. World needs more fossil fuel use, not less

August 24, 2015

The truth is the benefits to humans of the use of fossil fuels by creative, hardworking, enterprising humans are infinitely greater than any negatives in the past, in the present, and in the foreseeable future. Fossil fuels, coal, oil and gas produces 86% of the world's energy, is a boon to global agriculture, industry, transportation and a cornucopia of essential products. Unfortunately, billions of our neighbors, and their numbers are growing, have a desperate need for food, shelter, clothing, medicines, clean water, etc. and are urgently in need of greater energy to produce them. Greatly expanding the global use of fossil fuels is essential to provide such energy.

Global fossil fuels accessible reserves are dependent on continuing development of new technologies, market conditions, and now in the 21st century very much on governmental restrictions. The United States has the greatest known coal reserves in the world. It is our most abundant, reliable and least expensive energy source. China's coal reserves are also enormous, 3rd

behind Russia and the US and is building 2 coal-fired power plants a week, equivalent every year to the UK's total power grid. The United States success with shale oil and gas is not just a national, but also a global, game changer. Removing unreasonable restrictions to known accessible oil and natural gas reserves in the US Continental shelf and Alaska would add enormously to US reserves. The completion of the Keystone pipeline from Canada would add further. Given the right decisions by the US government and aggressive, responsible entrepreneurial effort by the private sector the US could be assured of sufficient fossil fuel availability well into the next century.

The environmental ideologues, the "anti-fossil fuelers", Al Gore, Johann Schellnhuber, B. K. Moon, the United Nation's global bureaucracy, UNIPCC, UNCGG, UNFCC, UNEP to name only a few and their sycophants in their blatant power grab have been modeling and predicting apocalyptic disasters due to manmade global warming for decades and have been proven wrong for decades. They are operating on the principle whoever controls the world's energy controls the world.

The latest Remote Sensing Systems (RSS) report states there has been no global warming in the past 18 and half years, yet UN climate models have been predicting steeply rising temperatures for the past two decades. However, these repeated failures have not deterred them from their goal of using the false issue of MMGW as the leverage to gain global governance. The United Nations Commission on Global Governance (UNCGG) believes the concept of national sovereignty, as a principle will yield steadily and reluctantly to the new imperative of global environmental cooperation and that global governance is increasingly relevant to achieving "sustainable development". The United Nations creation, Agenda 21, purpose is to further a key Socialist goal of international redistribution of wealth under the shibboleth of "sustainable development". Its immediate goal is to gain "global authority" to centralize/control, eliminate "without delay" the use of fossil fuels.

President Obama is joined with the "anti-fossil fuelers" and is implementing Agenda 21's roadmap here in the United States, to, as he says, be a leader for the world to follow. The latest wrongheaded examples are his EPA's draconian attempts to redefine the "waters of the United States" (WOTUS) and also shut down coal fired power plants. Listen to the UN's Director Steiner of the United Nation Environmental Program (UNEP); "President Obama's plans are an important signal from the US in the run up to our December COP21 meeting in Paris". President Obama's actions, which mirror Agenda 21's rules, are already causing escalating energy costs, tyrannical takeover of property rights, loss of individual freedoms, and degradation of the economy. Fortunately, these unconstitutional actions are being challenged by dozens of states and leaders in Congress.

The unmet needs of billions of our neighbors (see above) are the problem not MMGW. The solutions require more global fossil fuels use, not less, more global free markets, not less, more global hard work, not less, more global individual creativity, enterprise and freedom, not less.

33. America- we have a problem (AWHAP)

December 2, 2015

The Global War on Terror (GWOT) includes, among many others, the atrocity of 9/11/2001 where hijacked airplanes crashed into the WTC, the Pentagon and the field in Pa. This act of war killed and injured many thousands of innocent people on that day. The numbers of dead and injured are being added to every day. Of course, there are untold numbers of relatives and friends who will carry the burden of the loss and suffering of their loved ones for the rest of their lives. Remember September 11, 2001. Who are these terrorists that committed this greatest act of war on America's homeland since Pearl Harbor? Remember December 7, 1941.

The bipartisan 9/11 Commission Report answers that question, quote, "But the enemy is not just "terrorism" some generic evil. The catastrophic threat is more specific. It is the threat posed by *Islamist Terrorism*. The *Islamist Terrorists* mean exactly what they say: America is the font of all evil, the 'head of the snake' and it must be converted or destroyed. It is not a position with which America can bargain or negotiate.

With it there is no common ground on which to begin a dialogue. Its purpose is to rid the world of religious and political pluralism, the plebiscite, and equal rights for women. It makes no distinction between military and civilian targets."

The *Islamist Terrorists* take their marching orders from Islam's Holy books, the Qur'an, Hadiths and Sharia Law. Prime Minister Erdogan of Turkey declares, "There is no moderate Islam, Islam is Islam."

President and CIC Obama not only refuses to name America's enemy in the GWOT, *Islamist Terrorism*, but has been derelict in his conduct of this war.

Let's take a quick look at how the GWOT is going under President Obama's watch;

- The last 6 full years of his watch (2009 thru 2014) domestic attacks average per year, 3.5 attacks, 7.5 people killed and 50.2 people injured. These attacks incl. Fort Hood (mil.), Little Rock (mil), and Boston (civ.)
- In the 6 years prior to his becoming President (2008 back to 2003) domestic
- Attacks averaged per year 1.5 attacks, 1.7 people killed, 2.7 people injured.

- As of 12/2, year 2015 total killed is now 19, nearly 3 times the avg. rate for
- Past 6 years. Add San Bernardino 14, Chattanooga 5
- The *Islamic* State (ISIS) rose under his watch. It now controls vast territory in
- Syria and Iraq and ISIS cells now spread across North Africa to the Middle East. It continues to kill, behead and otherwise persecute Christians with impunity.
- Cuts in military and related intel. have jeopardized readiness and morale.
- Our "thin blue line", the nation's police forces, the first responders are over stretched and under siege.
- Chairman Joint Chiefs General Dunford says we have not contained ISIS and

Strategically they have spread since 2010. Yet President Obama said just before the Paris attacks, ISIS is contained and "climate change" is the greatest threat to America

FBI Dir. Comey says we have launched ISIS related investigations in all 50 States. He adds ISIS is capable of cyberattacks against the U. S.

Yes, AWHAP. The problem is President Obama has been and is derelict in his sworn duty to "provide for the common defense". It is up to "We the People", Republicans, Democrats, Independents, non-aligned to demand that Congress and the Judiciary take whatever constitutional steps possible to limit further weakening of our national defense and economy during his remaining months in office and that President Obama with his military team develop a strategy to win the GWOT.

34. "Forming a more perfect Union"

December 30, 2015

As the United States of America stands on the threshold of the year 2016 it can look back with pride and gratitude over the past 239 years from its Declaration of Independence and its 228 years as a Constitutional Republic. It has weathered many a storm and achieved many victories. Certainly, the birth of our nation was a perilous and painful struggle, testing the courage and wisdom of our Patriots with no certainty of the final outcome. The period leading up to and through the Civil War was unquestionably the greatest threat to our UNION'S continued existence. It is this period that brought forth one of America's greatest Presidents Abraham Lincoln.

President Lincoln at his 1st Inaugural Address March 4, 1861 was standing on the threshold of the year 1861. The UNION, during prior years had been enduring tumultuous times on the issues of slavery, Westward expansion to name only a few. Lincoln of course had run for the Senate against Stephen Douglas during this very fractious time and although losing to Douglas had spoken out eloquently and passionately on the issues. His famous House Divided speech in 1858 where he said, "A house divided against itself cannot stand." Lincoln, during this chaotic period, fought for and won the Presidency in November 1860, secession of southern states followed. In his 1st Inaugural Address, "We are not enemies but friends. We must not be enemies. Though passion may have strained, it must not break our bonds of affection. The mystic chords of memory, stretching from every battlefield and patriot grave to every living heart and hearthstone all over this broad land, will yet swell the chorus of the UNION when again touched, as surely they will be by the better angels of our nature." On April 12, 1861 the Confederacy fired on the UN-ION'S garrison at Fort Sumter and the Civil War was on. The Civil War was won, at a terrible cost on both sides, by the UNION under President Lincoln's leadership and the UNION was saved.

As we look forward through 2016 and beyond our UNION, our Constitutional Republic is being assailed by existential threats both foreign and domestic. In order to continue, "to form a more perfect UNION" we the people should not only listen to Lincoln's words but also to those of the legendary poet of those times Henry Wadsworth Longfellow in his poem "The Republic".

Thou, too sail on, O Ship of State!

Sail on, O UNION, strong and great!

Humanity with all its fears,

With all the hopes of future years,

Is hanging breathless on thy fate!

We know what Master laid thy keel,

What Workmen wrought thy ribs of steel,

Who made each mast, and sail, and rope.

What anvils rang, what hammers beat,

In what a forge and what a heat

Were shaped the anchors of thy hope!

Fear not each sudden sound and shock,

'Tis of the wave and not the rock;

'Tis but the flapping of the sail,

And not a rent made by the gale!

In spite of rock and tempest's roar,

In spite of false lights on the shore,

Sail on, nor fear to breast the sea!

Our hearts, our hopes, are all with thee,

Our hearts, our hopes, our prayers, our tears,

Our faith triumphant o'er our fears,

Are all with thee – are all with thee!

35. "... A Republic if you can keep it."

April 1, 2016

The three founding documents of America are The Declaration of Independence (1776), The Constitution of the United States (1787), and The Bill of Rights (1791). The Constitution created a new federal government that would secure the independence and rights proclaimed in the other two documents.

It is reported as Benjamin Franklin left Independence Hall at the close of the Constitutional Convention in Sept. 1787, where he along with 54 others had worked and debated since May to create this new government, that a lady asked him, "Well Doctor, what have we got a Republic or a Monarchy?" Ben replied, "A Republic if you can keep it."

George Washington, 1st President – "This Constitution demonstrates as visibly the finger of Providence as any possible event in the course of human affairs." John Adams, 2nd President- "The Constitution is the greatest single effort of national deliberation that the world has ever seen."

Yes, The United States of America is a Constitutional Republic in which the members of the Legislature, Executive and Judicial branches are representatives of the people and are bound by the Constitution in their governance. This exceptional nation in its relatively short life has provided more opportunity, more of the good life for more people on this old globe than any other nation in the history of the world.

Election 2016 is perhaps the most consequential election in our nation's history. Our Constitutional Republic has been under attack by two existential forces. First, by anti-constitutional, secular progressive, socialist forces resulting in an erosion of our constitutional foundations. This erosion, this transformation has been accelerated under the leadership of President Obama and his Democrat followers. Second, by the global war brought on by Islamist Terrorists who get their marching orders from Islam's sacred texts, the Koran, Hadiths and Shariah Law. Under President Obama's watch there has been a sharp increase in the number of Islamist Terrorist attacks both domestic and foreign. There has been the emergence and growth of ISIS along with its horrific atrocities.

Presidential Election 2016 has been dominated recently by three Republican candidates, Ted Cruz,

John Kasich and Donald Trump and by two Democrat candidates, Hillary Clinton and Bernie Sanders. Donald Trump has been called today's P. T. Barnum, a successful showman (circus) of the 19th century, known as "Prince of Humbugs". Barnum quote, "The bigger the humbug, the better people like it." That rule may have worked for the shills on Barnum's midways but not for our 45th President. The nation must avoid replacing President Obama's humbug with Trump's, Clinton's and Sanders's humbug.

As stated earlier our Constitutional Republic, our ship of state is sailing in very troubled waters and is off course. When our 45th President takes the helm in January 2017 that person must be, one well grounded, heart, mind and soul in the constitutional principles set forth in America's three founding documents, one whose compass headings point to the course set by those documents, one who is outraged at the injuries, loss of life and property inflicted on Americans and others by these Islamist Terrorists as well as the cost and life style changes required to defend against them and one totally committed to leading this nation and its allies to the complete elimination of Islamist Terrorism ASAP.

That person is Ted Cruz. Go to www.tedcruz.org for his stand on all the issues. Vote for Ted Cruz in the Republican primary on April 19.

36. "...With a firm reliance on the protection of divine providence..."

June 12, 2016

America will celebrate on July 4th the 240th anniversary of its Declaration of Independence. This document proclaimed and justified the end of rule by King George III and the British over America. This document is the first of the three founding documents of the United States. The other two being the Constitution and the Bill of Rights.

The American Revolutionary War began April 19, 1775 by the British attack at the Battle of Lexington. After some early victories and many defeats, including the disastrous invasion of Canada in Dec. 1775, General George Washington found himself and his small army of Patriots fighting a losing battle in Long Island and New York against an armada of over 50 British warships in the New York harbor and over 40,000 veteran British soldiers and sailors. These massive British forces had been ordered by King George III to totally crush the colonial rebellion out of its existence. General Washington and his army escaped the British onslaught by retreating across the Hudson River into

New Jersey and across the Delaware River into Pennsylvania.

As American forces were under siege in New York in the summer of 1776, the delegates to the 2nd Continental Congress in Philadelphia were debating the wisdom of declaring independence, knowing they could be hung for treason if caught by the British.

After much debate, brilliant writing by its chief architect, Thomas Jefferson, a 33-year-old delegate from Virginia, editing by other delegates, the final document was approved and adopted on July 4, 1776. This document, after listing all the tyrannical "injuries and usurpations" by King George III, proclaimed in its final paragraph, "That these United Colonies are, and of Right ought to be Free and Independent States." Also, its final pledge. "And for the support of this Declaration, with a firm reliance on the protection of divine Providence, we mutually pledge to each other our Lives, our Fortunes and our sacred Honor."

The war was to continue for years. Victories, defeats, hardships yet to come were many, Washington crossing the Delaware (1776), Valley Forge (1777-78), Saratoga (1777), Charlestown, SC (1780), to name only a few. Ultimately America was victorious over the most powerful military in the world when the British surrendered at Yorktown, VA. On Oct. 19, 1781. However, hostilities did not completely cease until the Treaty of Paris in 1783. The war lasted over 8 years and had the highest casualty rate of any U. S. war; only the civil war was bloodier. The sacrifices and sufferings endured by the men, women and children of the civilian population were incredible.

Obviously, the Constitution (1787) and the Bill of Rights (1791) would not have been possible without the Declaration and winning the war for independence. The Bill of Rights specified the foundational rights of the American people, including the freedoms of religion, speech, press, assembly and petition. The Constitution formed a new, unique Federal government to protect these rights. As the Preamble states, "We the People of the United States, in Order to form a more perfect Union, establish Justice, insure domestic Tranquility, provide for the common defense, promote the general Welfare, and secure the blessings of Liberty to ourselves and our Posterity, do ordain and establish this Constitution for the United States of America."

❖

37. Pope Francis and MMGW

September 11, 2016

A recent letter writer has brilliantly expressed her opinion re Pope Francis's embrace and preaching on <u>Man Made Global Warming</u> (MMGW) even going so far as saying, "these are sins that we have not hitherto acknowledged and confessed." Her opinion is re-mindful of St. Augustine's quote, "one does not read in the gospel that the lord said: "I will send you a par-aclete who will teach you about the course of the sun and the moon. For he willed to make them Christians and not mathematicians." Pope Francis, it seems, with his collectivist approach has ignored pope John Paul II, a strong champion of free markets and individual freedom.

The ideological MMGW extremists Pope Francis uses as his advisors on the subject are the most ex-treme in the MMGW debate. People such as Joachim Schellnhuber epitomizes, not only their extreme radi-cal agendas, but some even contrary to catholic doc-trine. In addition, Pope Francis has relied on the unit-ed nations bureaucracy. These advisors goal is to es-tablish "global authority". Their slogan is "global to local". President Obama has joined with them in their false concepts re MMGW and is implementing their wrongheaded agenda here in the U.S., to, as he says be a leader for the world to follow.

The ideological MMGW extremists in their blatant power grab have been modeling, manipulating data and predicting apocalyptic disasters for decades and have been proven wrong for decades.

The world's unmet needs are the problem, not MMGW. The solutions require more of all sources of energy including fossil fuels, not less, more global free markets, not less, more global creative human actions, not less, more individual freedom, not less.

38. Countdown to election 2016

September 17, 2016

Voting choices made on November 8 will determine the direction our Federal and State governments will take in the years ahead. The two major political parties and their candidates present substantial differences in their platforms and how they will contend with the challenges ahead. The individual voter in the short time left needs to both learn these challenges and determine the candidate that best represents his/her views.

Voter turnout data from the United States Election Project for the 2012 Presidential election (www.electproject.org) reports the following: The Voter Eligible Population (VEP) was 222,474,111, there were 129,070,906 votes cast for a 58% turnout. This meant that 93,403,205 or 42% of citizens eligible to vote failed to vote. It will be another colossal voter turnout failure in 2016 if this dismal turnout result cannot be substantially improved.

Election 2016 is perhaps the most consequential election in our nation's history.

America, our Constitutional Republic is under attack from forces both domestic and foreign. Domestically by anti-constitutional, secular progressive, socialist forces resulting in a suppression of our economic and military strength and an erosion of our constitutional principles and values. Foreign, first and most immediate by the global war brought on by Islamist terrorists who get their marching orders from Islam's sacred texts, the Qur'an, Hadiths, and Sharia Law, and second the growing threats from China, Russia, Iran and North Korea.

There are two important documents specifying many issues and two clearly different directions in contending with these challenges. They are the 2016 Democrat Platform www.demconvention.com/platform and the 2016 Republican Platform www.GOP.com/platform. The former reflecting a status quo direction and the latter reflecting a change in direction. Individuals should study, discuss, debate these platforms and actively support those candidates who best represents their views as they prepare to vote on Tuesday, November 8, 2016.

The following is a list of just a few of the many issues obtained from the Republican Platform: economic growth, jobs, immigration (legal and illegal), energy (all sources, including coal, oil and natural gas), international trade, taxes, regulation (more than 90%of federal requirements are now imposed by regulating agencies without any vote of the House or Senate or signature of the President), national debt, judicial activism (need to appoint judges who respect the rule of law in the Constitution), protect religious liberty, the unborn, traditional marriage, health care (repeal and replace Obamacare), social security, Medicare, Medicaid, limited government (Federalism is the cornerstone of our constitutional system per 10th amendment- "Powers not delegated to the U. S. by the Constitution, nor prohibited by it to the States, are reserved to the States respectively, or to the people"), rebuild the military. See next paragraph.

The incredibly shrinking manpower and equipment, both conventional and 21st century, of all branches of our active military places our nation at great risk and requires urgent and substantial rebuilding in view of the growing military capabilities and aggressiveness of Russia, China, North Korea and Iran.

In addition, our Reserve and National Guard forces need substantial rebuilding. There is an urgent need to correct our Veterans Administration inability to provide acceptable service to our veterans. President George Washington, "To be prepared for war is one of the most effective means of preserving the peace."

39. Letter to Catholic Courier for articles in 10/24/16 edition

October 24, 2016

From one of Hillary Clinton's "irredeemable (not capable of redemption) deplorables". The huge story out of the Al Smith dinner was the subject of abortion; protection of the unborn was spoken of from the podium in front of thousands of dinner guests and 10s of millions of TV viewers. Let's expand the discussion. Donald Trump and the Republican platform support protection for the unborn, Hillary Clinton and the Democrat platform support unlimited abortion-on-demand. Donald Trump will appoint Supreme court justices who will protect the constitutional right to life of the unborn, Hillary Clinton will appoint Supreme Court justices who will protect women's right for "reproductive choice" (abortion). Donald Trump is opposed to taxpayer funding of abortion and supports the Hyde amendment. Hillary Clinton supports taxpayer funding of abortions and wants to do away with the Hyde amendment.

The law banning Partial Birth abortion was passed in 2003 by a large majority of Republicans in the

House and Senate, opposed by a large majority of Democrats in both houses and signed by the Republican President. This law was declared constitutional by the SCOTUS in 2007. Senator Hillary Clinton was one of the many Democrats who voted against this bill. Donald Trump supports this bill, Hillary Clinton still opposes this bill.

Because of many 21st century scientific/medical breakthroughs, truly miraculous medical interventions are accomplished, such as fetal surgery. Because it has been established the baby in the womb experiences pain at 20 weeks gestation and even earlier fetal anesthesia is routinely administered. Question: Does Planned Parenthood use fetal anesthesia when they harvest the baby's organs for resale?

The Pain Capable Unborn Child Protection Act HR 36 has been passed by the House, a large majority of Republicans voted for passage, a large majority of Democrats voted against passage. A large majority of Senate Republicans 51 voted for passage but a large majority of Senate Democrats 40 voted against passage making it fall short of the 60 votes necessary to block a Democrat filibuster. Donald Trump supports this bill. Hillary Clinton opposes this bill and supports abortion of a full-term baby.

Final question: How can the Democrat Presidential candidate Hillary Clinton and the Democrat party continue to support abortion-on-demand, defend the indefensible, now in the 21st century?

40. Greatest upset in America's political history

December 2, 2016

The United States of America, our Constitutional Republic, has just had a seismic historic election with a mandate for change. The Republican President-elect Donald Trump's win over Democrat Sec. Hillary Clinton, despite his never having run for public office, with Republican establishment leaders opposed to his candidacy and the Democrat candidate being supported by a united Democrat party, over a billion campaign dollars, a sycophantic media, Hollywood, and academia, was truly a shocking result for the 2016 Presidential election.

There are many reasons for this; generally, the losing side has ranted, over and over, their loss was due to racism, prejudice and hatred. Clearly an emotional response of sore losers, without foundation in fact. I suggest they read Booker T. Washington's famous Atlanta Compromise speech in 1895 when he said, "Cast down your bucket where you are", and gave invaluable guidance both to members of his own race and to members of the white race. For those sore losers, just for the record, overwhelmingly most people in America are concerned about having a job in order to support their family and to secure for them and neighbors the "unalienable rights of life, liberty and the pursuit of happiness". They are not racists or haters. Let's look at just some of the factual reasons for the historic win.

The secular progressives have taken over today's Democrat party. This election has established that our Constitutional Republic is opposed to such an agenda. Today's Democrat party is in disarray and now huddled in a defensive crouch in the extreme liberal states of the Northeast and the West Coast. Today's Republican party now represents the movement toward a moral and religious nation, based on Judeo-Christian and Constitutional values/principles. As our 2nd President, John Adams, said, "Our Constitution was made only for a moral and religious people. It is wholly inadequate to the government of any other."

This movement, plus the Republican goals, to name only a few, of lower taxes, less regulation, limited government, controlled legal immigration, stop illegal immigration, more production of coal, oil and natural gas, opposition to "global governance" (see

COP 21) of energy, protection of the unborn, traditional marriage and religious liberty, control national
debt, appoint constitutional/conservative justices to
the SCOTUS, rebuild the military, strong defense
against the enemy of Islamist Terrorism and other potential enemies, improve international trade deals,
combined with outstanding candidates at the Federal
and State levels resulted in the amazing win.

The New York Times reports as of Nov. 29, 2016
the delegate count for President was 306 for Trump
and 232 for Clinton. According to ballotpedia.org as
America enters the year 2017 Republicans will control
the Presidency and both houses of Congress. There
will be 31 States with a Republican Governor, 37 with
a Republican Senate and 31 with a Republican House.
States with Trifecta Governments (one party control
for Governor, Senate & House) in the year 2010 were
10 with a Repub. Trifecta & 17 with a Demo. Trifecta.
Now as we enter 2017 there will be 25 States with a
Repub. Trifecta and only 6 with a Demo. Trifecta.

Clearly Republicans, at the Federal and State levels, dominate the political leadership of our Constitutional Republic. Even so they will need to seek and
welcome cooperation from non-Republicans wherev-

er possible. Theirs is a great responsibility and a heavy burden, not only to achieve their promised goals, but to "preserve, protect and defend the Constitution of the United States" and the "unalienable rights" of all the people.

41. 2017, Expect more protections for the unborn

January 16, 2017

The 43rd annual March for Life will be held in Washington DC on January 27th. This events purpose is to celebrate the beauty of life, the dignity of each human person, support protections for the unborn and memorialize the victims of the infamous Roe v Wade Supreme Court decision on 1/22/73. Since this exercise of "Raw Judicial Power" (per dissenting Justice Byron White) by the SCOTUS making abortions legal in all 50 states there have been over 60 million unborn children killed by abortion.

During the current Senate confirmation hearings for President-Elect Trump's nominees the subject of Roe v Wade is frequently being discussed confirming its continuing high national priority. The SCOTUS legalized abortion under RvW on a "right to privacy" that it "found" in the 14th amendment and in doing so it said the state had an interest in protecting the unborn child that increased as pregnancy progressed. Justice Harry Blackmun, writing the majority opinion in the last century, said, "We need not resolve the difficult question of when life begins." Now in the 21st century scientific and medical advances inform us that by 8 weeks after fertilization the baby in the womb has every organ in place, reacts to touch, begins to hear and experiences pain no later than 20 weeks, perhaps earlier. Increasingly the unborn child is being treated as a patient with fetal surgery evolving into a more mainstream form of treatment, including the use of fetal anesthesia.

Because of this continuing increase in knowledge of the unborn, legal protections at the state and federal levels have continued to grow. The Partial-Birth Abortion Ban Act (PBA) after years of effort was finally passed and found constitutional by the SCOTUS in 2007. PBA, conducted in the last months of pregnancy, is a gruesome and inhumane procedure, crosses the line from abortion to infanticide. Many Democrats in Congress opposed and voted against this ban. Another legal protection passed by the House (supported by Republicans opposed by Democrats), currently being blocked by Democrats in the Senate is the Pain-Capable Unborn Child Protection Act. This protection prohibits abortion after 20 weeks and should become law in 2017.

House speaker Republican Paul Ryan just announced that Congress will defund Planned Parenthood (PP) in 2017. The PP fiscal 2014 report states the number of abortions performed for the year by the organization were 327,653. That would make PP the largest abortion provider in the nation at over 30% of est. annual abortions of 1,058,000. The House Select investigative panel released its final 471-page report on Jan 4, saying PP is guilty of breaking numerous state and federal laws in their criminal harvesting and sale of aborted baby parts urging Congress to halt federal payments to PP. Senator Grassley, Chairman of the Senate Judiciary Comm. following its investigation has referred PP to the FBI and the Dept. of Justice for further investigation and possible prosecution.

Encouragingly reports show that America's abortion numbers are declining in recent years. Obviously, there are many reasons for this; some suggest that one of them being beliefs, values and abortion culture are changing brought about by the greater knowledge of the unborn. Is it possible that in the near future an enlightened majority of the SCOTUS would decide the baby in the womb is a person and is protected by the 14th amendment?

42. Senator Schumer turns back on upstate voters

February 19, 2017

Your Sunday 2/19 edition was devoted to your continuing Anti-Trump stand. Three headlined articles, took up the front page, "Resist Trump", "Trump, bipartisan pushback" and "Trump renews old insults". These were continued on pages A6, A7 and A8 with pictures of protesters holding signs saying "Dump Trump" etc. Page A9, an editorial continuing the same message. These articles also charged, early Trump supporters, Congressmen Chris Collins and Tom Reed (who easily won their districts) with ignoring their constituents and failing to represent them on what is going on in Washington and in their home districts. Your paper has largely avoided reporting on New York State Democrat Senator Schumer's wrongheaded leadership in obstructing, slowing down, stopping President Trump's agenda, on his ignoring & failure to represent millions of upstate New York citizens who voted for President Trump and the Republican agenda. Let's look at the record:

Hillary Clinton defeated Donald Trump by 1,736,590 votes in all of New York State (NY Times Feb 10, 2017). Hillary Clinton won by 1.737,450 votes in just 5 New York Metropolitan counties Brooklyn, Queens, Manhattan, Bronx and Nassau with 78% of the vote. Manhattan and the Bronx alone voted 90% in favor of Clinton. Donald Trump won 45 Upstate New York counties. Ontario County, combined with Wayne, Livingston, Seneca, Yates, Steuben and Schuyler voted 61% for Donald Trump, 39% for Hillary Clinton. Is it possible the Daily Messenger with its Anti-Trump message is doing a disservice to 61% of the voters in this area?

Senator Schumer now recognized as the pseudo national leader of the leaderless Democrat party has embraced the secular progressives in the New York City area and across the nation. He has conducted, boycotts of nominee hearings, filibustered and pledged to fight "tooth & nail" to prevent President Trump and the Republican agenda from succeeding. Despite this juggernaut of opposition from the Democrat (NO) party and the Main Stream Media (MSM), President Trump and the Republican Party under his leadership have achieved a record number of substantial accomplishments, including excellent nominees for his cabinet and the U. S. Supreme Court.

Suggestion to the Daily Messenger, next Sunday 2/26 objectively/factually report on the long list of President Trump's accomplishments in his 1st month in office as well as by the Republican House and Senate. Many of these to fix problems, as promised, created by the Obama Administration.

America is indeed fortunate to have had President Trump win along with the Republicans winning the House and the Senate. They are going to need all support possible for the next 4 years and beyond. Those who voted for Donald Trump and his agenda, Republicans, Democrats and independents make your voices heard by whatever constitutional means available to you.

43. Obamacare, mendacity personified

May 6, 2017

Obamacare is a false concept, promoted by President Obama and his Democrat followers with blatant mendacity. Obamacare is a power grab by the Executive Branch to take over 1/6 of the U. S. economy, to micro-manage the nation's health care from Washington, to take control over the medical decisions of individuals and their doctors. Examples of the lies and failures of Obamacare are strewn across America's landscape, visible to all with eyes and ears willing to see and hear.

Obamacare, the Affordable Care Act (ACA) mandates all individuals must buy health insurance, either thru an employer or other source, anyone not doing so has to pay a penalty (tax rising each year). The purpose being that those having lower cost medical needs (the younger, healthier) would pay for those having higher cost medical needs (the older, less healthy). The ACA mandates each policy must have "essential health benefits" whether insured wants or needs them. The recently House-passed American Health Care Act HR1628 eliminates Obamacare's mandates and provides block grants to those states that want to establish "high risk pools" for the higher cost individuals.

Obamacare premiums are increasing at unsustainable rates, as are deductibles, insurance carriers are dropping out of the system. See "Shaky Obamacare Market Adds to 'Death Spiral' Fears" by Tatiana Darie 9/23/16 Bloomberg: "Most of the 23 Obamacare created non-profit co-op insurers have failed…more on the brink of folding…the situation looks dire… large insurers including Aetna and United Health have pulled back from Obamacare markets."

The largest of these 23 Obamacare co-op insurers was Health Republic Insurance of New York, a tragic poster-child for Obamacare failures. It went bankrupt in late 2015 causing over 200,000 insureds, after many frustrating and painful struggles trying to get their claims paid, to lose their insurance. In addition, hundreds of millions were owed to medical providers, doctors, hospitals, others. HRINY's failure resulted in complete chaos for its former customers and their medical providers. HRINY has been in the process of a complicated, costly (lots of lawyers), lengthy liquidation now for the past year. Apparently, no individuals, those directly in charge, in the New York State Insurance Dept., (DFS) or the management of HRINY have been held accountable for this colossal failure.

There is no question Obamacare must be repealed and replaced. Kudos to those Republicans in the House who have made a major beginning on eliminating the abomination of Obamacare by passing HR1628. The battle now goes to the Senate.

Unfortunately, prominent Democrat voices of today's leaderless Democrat party are now using the same techniques of inflammatory, demagogic, mendacious rhetoric they used during their creation of Obamacare to prevent the elimination of Obamacare.

It is up to Republicans, Independents and those remaining Democrats who believe in individual freedom and constitutional principles to persevere, to follow President Trump's lead and finally repeal and replace Obamacare this year.

❖

44. 72nd Anniversary V-J Day August 14, 1945

July 20, 2017

On December 7, 1941 the Imperial Japanese Navy (IJN) using 6 of its aircraft carriers and hundreds of aircraft launched a sneak attack on the United States by bombing the U. S. Navy ships and personnel at Pearl Harbor, Hawaii. This "Day of Infamy", as President Roosevelt called it was devastating with over 3,500 Americans killed or injured, and many ships/planes sunk, destroyed or heavily damaged. Japan's war against the United States had begun. Germany as a member of the Axis powers declared war on the United States on Dec. 11, 1941. World War II was now official. Remember Pearl Harbor!

America was confronted with a two-front war, the European-Atlantic (E-A) and the Asia-Pacific (A-P). President Roosevelt focused most of America's limited resources on the E-A theatre but also began the difficult, brutal and bloody land, sea and air battles to defeat Japan. The entire A-P war alone from 1941 thru 1945 cost hundreds of thousands of American and allied deaths, injuries, POWs and MIAs with great sacrifices on the Home Front.

By early 1942 the Axis powers had conquered a large part of the world. Germany/Italy had North Africa, Europe/France and were poised to invade England. Japan had Manchuria, much of Southeast Asia, Philippines, much of China, the Western Pacific and was on its way to invade Australia.

The Japanese people were united under the ultra-nationalistic State Shinto religion from pre-WWII until 1945. State Shinto doctrine included, Emperor Hirohito's sovereignty was exercised by divine right, the Japanese people were superior to other peoples, Japan's unlimited expansion, the suppression of individual freedoms and democratic principles. Japan's leaders convinced their troops and the nation that it was a greater humiliation to surrender to the enemy than to die. Suicide was an honorable final action.

Under the unconditional surrender terms in 1945 all government sponsorship of State Shinto was abolished; individual freedoms and democratic principles were instituted.

Japan, during their wars of expansion begun in the 1930s, committed thousands of horrendous atrocities such as the "Rape of Nanking" in 1937, the "Bataan Death March" in 1942. Emperor Hirohito sanctioned the policy to "Kill all, burn all, loot all" causing the deaths of millions of Chinese. Japan's War Ministry issued an edict that all POWs were to be killed by any means necessary. War crimes trials found many of Japan's leaders guilty and sentenced to death or life in prison.

The leaders of Japan knowing America was going to invade their Homeland developed a fanatical, suicidal defense plan called Operation Ketsugo (OK). OK mobilized and trained civilians to defend their Homeland along with the military. Japan was not going to surrender.

America's invasion plan was called Operation Downfall (OD). Approved in early 1945 after considering other options such as blockades and continued air bombardment. This land, sea and air invasion was to be by far the largest such invasion in history, many times larger than D-day Normandy and was to begin November 1, 1945. The Joint Chiefs estimated OD would result in over a million American and allied casualties and several million Japanese casualties. Operation Downfall was the invasion that never happened.

President Truman (President since April, 1945 upon President Roosevelt's death) called for Japan's unconditional surrender in July 1945, implementing President Roosevelt's 1943 Doctrine of Unconditional Surrender for all Axis powers. Japan refused. President Truman made the decision to drop the 1st atomic bomb on Hiroshima on August 6. 1945. He again called for Japan's surrender. Japan again refused. President Truman dropped the 2nd atomic bomb on August 9, 1945. On August 14, 1945 President Truman announced Japan's unconditional surrender. Americans and the world took to the streets to celebrate. World War II, called "history's greatest catastrophe" was now over. America will always be grateful to those, military and civilian, who served. Remember V-J Day!

45. U.S. guided missile warships in demolition derby in Asian pacific

August 29, 2017

Guided missile warships are multi-role warships used in anti-submarine, anti-missile defense and intelligence gathering, a critical part of defense against North Korea and elsewhere. They contain the most sophisticated electronic/computer applications including radar.

JAN. 31, 2017 USS Antietam, guided missile cruiser ran aground in Tokyo bay, no injuries, heavily damaged, had to be towed to Navy base in Yokosuka, Japan.

MAY 9, 2017 USS Lake Champlain, guided missile cruiser was rammed on its port side by a South Korean fishing vessel in waters east of the Korean Peninsula, no injuries, damaged but still operable.

JUNE 17, 2017 USS Fitzgerald, guided missile destroyer, highly maneuverable was struck on its starboard side by a cargo ship south of Japan, 7 sailors killed, severe damage, had to be towed to U. S. Navy base in Yokosuka, Japan for extensive repairs.

AUGUST 19, 2017 USS John S McCain, guided missile destroyer, highly maneuverable, in collision with a merchant ship east of Singapore, 10 sailors killed, heavily damaged, had to be towed by tug to the Changi Naval Base in Singapore for extensive repairs.

The U. S. Navy announced immediately after each of these disastrous events that an investigation was initiated. We are now in the month of September. Where are the results of these investigations? What corrective actions are being taken?

Naval analyst Bryan Clark of Center for Strategic & Budgetary Assessment states, "… As the total number of ships operating over the last decade has gone down, the operational tempo has remained the same or increased. Fleet training has been reduced 20 to 25% over the last decade. There is a systemic problem overall that the surface Navy is getting worked a lot harder than it's been designed to do."

Adm. William Moran, the vice chief of naval operations before the House Armed Services Committee Feb. 7, "It has become clear to me that the Navy's overall readiness has reached the lowest level in many years."

GAO reports that from 2011 through 2014 only 28% of all scheduled maintenance was completed on time and only 11% on carriers,

The foregoing epitomizes the serious challenges faced not only by the U. S. Navy but also by America's other military branches. For example: The DOD reports the Marine Corps not only has a shortage of aircraft for wartime but for training. The Air Force reports it is short 1500 pilots and 3400 aircraft maintainers. Gen. Mark Milley, Army Chief of Staff tells the Senate, "The Army needs an active component of 540,000 to 550,000. The active component is now 476,000." This statement reflects the continued troop cuts since 2010 when the component stood at 570,000.

President Trump, in his Administration's budget for fiscal 2018 (his first as President) proposes a substantial increase in military spending. Congress has yet to act.

It's long past time for the American people, for Congress to recognize that we are engaged in a global war brought on by the Islamist terrorists, are under constant threat by nuclear powers Iran and North Korea and our reduced military capabilities, not only places our military men and women at greater risk but also our nation.

46. North Korea & Iran: Anti-US, Anti-Israel, Anti-West Partners

October 10, 2017

Kim Jong Un, the dictator of communist North Korea has proven to be a powerful, ruthless tyrant following in the footsteps of his father Kim Jong Il and his grandfather Kim Il Sung. This "family" has dictatorially ruled NK for seven decades and is infamous for its reigns of terror both within NK for its tens of thousands of executions and purges as well as for Kim Il Sung beginning the Korean war by his military invasion of South Korea across the 38th parallel in 1950. The U. S. under the UN flag joined in the defense of South Korea. After 3 years of war and millions of casualties, including 200,000 American casualties with 54,000 killed and 12,000 MIA and POW, a cease-fire was signed in 1953. A peace treaty has never been signed; in fact, in March 2013 NK declared the 1953 armistice invalid.

Under the Kims, NK is the most hardened communist state in the world, a totalitarian, atheist state that denies individual freedoms and has resulted in the impoverishment of its people. The Kims' driving motivation is to retain their power and control, one key element is to continuously convince the North Korean people that America, Israel and the West are evil and want to destroy NK. Now in the 21st century NK's current evil leader, Kim Jong Un has intercontinental missiles and nuclear bombs. He has been using these powerful weapons to threaten/blackmail America, thereby gaining support from his people and also blackmailing the U. S. into paying ransom for its protection. America, by President Clinton's "Agreed Framework" with NK in 1994 did just that. Subsequently NK was found violating the terms of the agreement. History shows that those who try appeasing, bribing or caving in to such tyrants proves fatal.

Ayatollah Ali Khamenei, the Supreme Leader for the past 28 years of Iran is God's representative on earth and has absolute power. Iran is an Islamic theocracy, governed by Sharia law, whose foreign policy is virulently anti-US, anti-Israel, and anti-West. Iran, like North Korea threatens America and Israel with annihilation by nuclear bombs and like NK has blackmailed the U. S. into paying ransom for protection.

President Obama's deeply flawed nuclear agreement with Iran, the Joint Comprehensive Plan of Action (JCPOA), was not only sweetened with illicit ransom payments of billions of dollars but also biased in Iran's favor. Iran is in significant violations of JCPOA including refusing to permit inspections of military sites, retaining outside access to nuclear technology and continuing to sponsor global Islamist terrorism.

National Review 8/31/17, Matthew Brodsky "The North Korean Axis of Middle East Proliferation": Reuters revealed a confidential UN report evidencing NK nefarious role in spreading weapons of mass destruction and missile technology to other rogue regimes such as Iran and Syria. The report highlights the extent NK has been a principal partner of Iran.

U. S. lawmakers passed overwhelmingly H.R.3364 the Countering America's Adversaries Act, signed by President Trump on Aug. 2, 2017 blunting the complimentary ambitions of Iran and NK, restricting Iranian & NK efforts to share missile, nuclear and weapons technology.

47. Respect and unite under America's flag and anthem

December 4, 2017

America has provided more opportunity, more individual freedom, more of the good life, for more people on this old globe than any other nation in recorded history. This accomplishment required much love, hard creative work, suffering and "a firm reliance on the protection of divine Providence." Yes, when the nation's flag is flown and its anthem played stand up with respect and gratitude for this great nation.

Does this mean America is a perfect nation? Of course not. It is a nation created, developed and defended by imperfect men and women and it isn't "done" yet. Much as each person is imperfect so too is America imperfect. However, it is essential to recognize and be grateful for what is right with America and to support its founding principles and values in order to be able to correct what is wrong with America.

The nation's flag and anthem symbolize what is right with America. When they are displayed and played in parades or elsewhere they make the people feel proud and united. For example, in America's sports arenas just before the game begins it is an opportunity for the team's players and supporters to unite in honor and respect for the symbols of what is right with America. Of course, this unity will be set aside as soon as the competition starts and rightly so but hopefully return at games end even if it takes a special effort if you're on the losing side.

There are many songs that give honor and respect to the United States of America. One of the most famous was written in 1862 by George Root "Battle Cry of Freedom" also called "Rally 'round the Flag". A great version by Ian Berwick is on you tube. The music and lyrics are inspirational. Abraham Lincoln used it in his 1864 campaign in support of the Union and abolition. It's been used in many venues including the Ken Burns documentary "The Civil War"

The music and lyrics of "The Star-Spangled Banner" also inspire. The last stanza perhaps says it best:

O, thus be it ever when freemen stand,

Between their lov'd homes and the war's desolation;

Blest with vict'ry and peace, may the heav'n-rescued land

Praise the Pow'r that hath made and preserv'd us a nation!

Then conquer we must, when our cause is just,

And this be our motto: "In God is our trust"

And the Star-Spangled Banner in triumph shall wave

O'er the land of the free and the home of the brave!

America has prevailed over many challenges, including many brutal and bloody wars during its relatively brief 240 years. To recall just one December 7, 1941, World War II. Today America and its founding principles are being attacked by powerful external and internal forces. Externally, military and economic, just to mention a few, Islamist Terrorism, North Korea, China, Russia. Internally those who would move America in a secular progressive direction away from its founding values, principles of individual freedom and constitutional republic. The American people need to respect and unite under the flag and anthem as they did in past crises. As President Lincoln said, "A house divided against itself cannot stand."

Made in the USA
San Bernardino, CA
07 November 2018